—AMILTON DISTRICT:
A History

Edited by
ina Burns, Alison Reid and Isabel Walker

HAMILTON
DISTRICT COUNCIL

HAMILTON DISTRICT COUNCIL 1995

© Hamilton District Council 1995

Published by Hamilton District Libraries

British Library Cataloguing-in-Publication-Data
A Catalogue record for this book is available from the British Library

ISBN 0 9501983 7 4

This book was typeset and produced in Scotland
by EM-DEE Productions, Glasgow

CONTENTS

5   Preface - *Provost Robert Newberry*
7   Introduction - *Alison Reid*
18   Hamilton - *Joyce J R Brown*
29   A Description of Hamilton - *Brown's Hamilton Directory, 1855*
31   A Walk Around Hamilton - *William Wallace*
41   The Good Old Burgh Town - *Anon*
42   The Hamilton Estate - *Sharon Paton*
53   An Excursion to the High Parks - *Anon*
55   Blantyre - *Neil Gordon*
67   Black Agnes - *Anon*
69   David Livingstone - *Scottish National Memorial to David Livingstone Trust*
78   An Extract from his "Missionary Travels" - *David Livingstone*
79   Uddingston - *David Jamieson*
90   Bothwell Castle - *Sir Walter Scott*
92   Bothwell - *Russell Thomson*
103   Bothwell Bank - *Anon*
105   Hamilton and the Covenanting Tradition - *William Niven*
114   Notes on Edinburgh - *Robert Louis Stevenson*
115   The Cameronians (Scottish Rifles) - *Alison Reid*
127   An Acrostik Upon His Name - *Anon*
128   Larkhall - *John Milligan and Helen Sykes*
140   Larkha' Bonnie Lassies - *Andrew Fisher*
141   The Story of the Textile Industry in Hamilton District - *Terry F Mackenzie*
153   The Weavers' Stone - *Terry F Mackenzie*
154   Quarter & Limekilnburn - *Julia Bearne*
163   Colin's Hot Blast - *A.H.*
164   The Story of the Mining Industry in Hamilton District - *Robert A Clark & Sharon A Martin*
175   Miner's Morning Song - *David Wingate*
177   Stonehouse - *Stonehouse Heritage Group*
187   Stonehouse Violet - *William McCoubrey*
188   Bibliography

HAMILTON DISTRICT

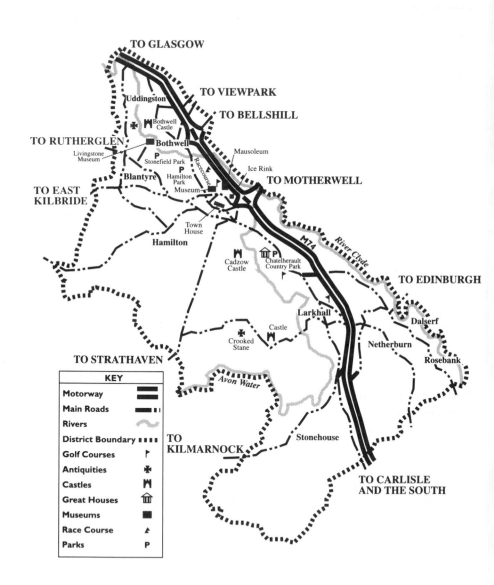

TO GLASGOW

TO VIEWPARK

Uddingston

TO BELLSHILL

Bothwell
Castle

TO RUTHERGLEN   Bothwell

Mausoleum

Livingstone
Museum

Stonefield Park

Ice Rink

Blantyre   Hamilton
Park

TO MOTHERWELL

TO EAST
KILBRIDE

Museum

Racecourse

Town
House

Hamilton

M74

River Clyde

Cadzow
Castle

Chatelherault
Country Park

TO EDINBURGH

Larkhall

Dalserf

Castle

Crooked
Stane

Netherburn

Rosebank

TO STRATHAVEN

Avon Water

TO
KILMARNOCK

Stonehouse

TO CARLISLE
AND THE SOUTH

KEY

Motorway	▬
Main Roads	▬ ▪
Rivers	∿
District Boundary	▪▪▪▪
Golf Courses	⚑
Antiquities	✳
Castles	♜
Great Houses	🏛
Museums	■
Race Course	⚑
Parks	P

4

PREFACE

In 1975, the reorganisation of local government created Hamilton District, an area of Lanarkshire stretching from Uddingston in the north to Stonehouse in the south, and bounded on its eastern side by the River Clyde. Within its fifty one square miles, Hamilton District has a wide variety of towns and villages, each with its own particular characteristics and history and each set in a different landscape moulded by that community's past. The handsome villas of Bothwell and Uddingston are reminders that these were once dormitory towns for the wealthy merchants of Glasgow, the weavers' cottages of Stonehouse reflect the former extent of this industry in the area and the observant eye can still pick out traces of the spoil heaps from the coal mines, now carefully landscaped and planted. It is the aim of this book to record the story of Hamilton District, whether for visitors from overseas, researchers looking for an introduction to the area or for local people who would like to know more about their own community.

Our book, however, is not simply a celebration of Hamilton District. It also marks a milestone in local government, for on 31 March, 1996, we will say good-bye to Hamilton District as we join with our neighbours, the surrounding areas of East Kilbride, Clydesdale, Rutherglen and Cambuslang, to form the new authority of South Lanarkshire. In this partnership we foresee the various strengths of the constituent communities complementing one another to achieve a highly effective and successful unitary authority. Our future achievements will, however, be created on the building-blocks of the past – the fertile farmland, the prosperity created from the spinning and the weaving, the coal, and then the spirit that enabled the people to regenerate and diversify when the traditional sources of industry had all dried up. On the eve of the inception of South Lanarkshire it is appropriate to look forward to a new beginning but also to pause for a moment, and reflect on those people and communities who make up our heritage.

This book has been created out of the enthusiasm of local people who have dug deep into the history of their towns and villages and recorded it for generations to come. Special thanks go to the following:- Julia Bearne, Joyce J R Brown, Robert A Clark, Neil Gordon, David Jamieson, Col. Ian McBain, Phil McCaffrey, Lt. Col. Hugh Mackay and the Cameronian (Scottish Rifles) Regimental Trustees, Terry F Mackenzie,

Provost Robert Newberry

Sharon A Martin, John Milligan, William Niven, Sharon Paton, The Scottish National Memorial to David Livingstone Trust, Stonehouse Heritage Group, Helen Sykes, Russell Thomson and William Wallace. I would also like to thank Eleanor Thomson for permission to use her late husband's work as a basis for the chapter on Bothwell. Finally, my thanks go to the editorial team of Diana Burns, Alison Reid and Isabel Walker, without whose drive and enthusiasm this project would never have materialised.

Our book is an anthology of the histories of individual communities and the ties that bind them together. It is impossible to divide areas or themes into neat chapters when a broader story is being told – the strands of weaving and the seams of coal and their impact on the people are covered in complimentary parts of several chapters, and the reader is encouraged to browse widely across the contents to enjoy the full flavour of the local tradition!

For some, this book will be the catalyst to start looking deeper into their own heritage, for others it will be a chance to reminisce over bygone times. Whatever this book is for you, I wish you enjoyment in reading it!

Provost Robert Newberry
Hamilton District Council

INTRODUCTION

by Alison Reid

Background

Hamilton District lies along the west bank of the River Clyde as it flows north from its source in the Leadhills to the Firth beyond Glasgow. The boundaries of the District follow the Clyde and Avon Valleys from Rosebank and Netherburn in the south to Uddingston in the north, rising from river level to over 500 feet.

The south has a soft, rural landscape with fertile meadow and orchard country along the riverside, rising to the higher grounds and pastures towards Strathaven to the west, while the north is a heavily populated industrial, commercial and residential zone. The population today is around 105,000, but all man-made boundaries are transient, and the pattern of settlement follows older divisions. These relate to the location of resources and their historic exploitation, which are shared with communities beyond the District boundaries.

There is nothing truly new under the sun, and the names we use to define political and administrative areas come, go, and return over the centuries, for the bonds between people and their land are rooted deep in the community's memory.

Hamilton District took its name from the burgh and town in 1975, and the burgh was named for the landowners, the Hamiltons, in 1455. Their name first appears in the 1290s with the barony of Cadzow, the earlier and first recorded name for this area. Strathclyde Region, which disappears along with Hamilton District in 1996, took its name from a kingdom of the early historic period, between around 500 and 1000 AD. The new authority of South Lanarkshire takes its name from the place name 'lanerc', also of the early historic period, and the 'shire' or sheriffdom, a royal administrative unit established by 1161 AD.

Physical Character

Hamilton District lies in what is geologically termed the Midland Valley of Scotland. This, in essence, is a 'Rift Valley' defined by fault lines along the Grampian Highlands to the north, and the Southern Uplands to the south. When these two fault lines shifted, the land between dropped and became, to some extent, sheltered by the tougher, older rock to

7

north and south. Later softer rock has been stripped from these by the action of ice and weathering, while the lower level of the valley protected it from the worst ravages.

The rocks immediately below our feet are primarily sedimentary rocks laid down as silt and decaying plants, and compressed over time. The two key periods for this area are the 'Old Red Sandstone' and 'Carboniferous' eras, which saw the creation of sandstone and coal beds. These have been squeezed and folded by the pressures on the two fault lines, and eroded by glacial action and weathering. This has left levels of useful minerals, particularly coal, layered between other rocks like lime, sand and ironstone, and mixed with poorer quality shale and clay.

Some of the coal seams are close to the surface, others deeply buried, and the human history of this area in recent centuries is tightly bound to their accessibility, and the advance of technology capable of accessing deeper beds.

The earliest attraction of the area, though, was not its minerals but its fertility. As the last glaciers melted, they left behind crushed rock and clay soils, to which were added the silts washed down from the higher ground by the water released from the ice. Streams and rivers carved channels through the rock – steep and fast through hard rock such as the Avon Gorge, and broad over the floodplains like the Clyde at Hamilton Low Parks. The land is still improved today by material washed down from higher ground by these drainage routes.

In addition to fertile soils, the area has the additional advantage of a mild climate and together these have given it a historic reputation not just for agriculture, but for fruit growing. This is recorded as early as the 700s by the Venerable Bede, from the monastery of Jarrow in Northumbria, when he writes of the 'appleyards of Lanark'.

Early Settlement

The earliest people here were nomads – hunter gatherers who moved with the food supply, exploiting whatever was to hand, around 6,000 years ago. Travelling mostly by water up the Clyde from the estuary or over the watershed from the Borders and Galloway, they built flimsy camps on the gravel beds by the river side, where the ground was dry and open. They fished the river, gathered wild fruits in season from the scrub woodland close by, and hunted deer and game in the thicker forest inland. Occasionally, scatters of worked or discarded flint flakes and tools are found, marking these temporary sites.

Somewhere between 5,000-4,000 years ago farming began. People learned how to clear areas of woodland by burning, which enriched the soil, and to plant and harvest grain, as well as domesticating wild animals. As the yield on each clearing dropped after a few years, new areas were opened up, and the settled population grew. Although little evidence remains of these early farms beyond occasional stone clearance cairns in upland areas, evidence of the development of communities with social and religious customs has been frequently found in single and group burials dating from around 3,500 years ago. These range from the massive cairn on Tinto Hill to single cist burials at Ferniegair and cremation urns at Blantyre.

As the population grew, so did pressure on usable land. From around 3,000 years ago, hill forts start to be built, reflecting either a religious or warrior aristocracy, as well as complex inter tribal trading and political relationships. The most impressive remains are in the hills of Clydesdale at sites like Arbory Hill and Black Hill, reflecting the importance of controlling the fertile valley for its food, and its importance as a communication route. Lowland forts are known too, at Camp Knowe in Blantyre or the possible fort in Chatelherault Park.

The Romans recognised the significance of the Clyde valley for communications on their first foray into Scotland in the 80s AD, and used it in each successive invasion, with a roadway north up the valley, and another branching off along the Avon valley towards the Ayrshire coast. Remains of the fort and bathhouse at Bothwellhaugh can still be visited today. The Roman presence was, however, at best intermittent, and probably had little effect on the lives of the native population. Nevertheless, the Romans do give us a picture of general tribal groupings such as the Damnonii of the Lower Clyde area, which were to emerge within a few centuries into sub-kingdoms, with named kings and outline histories, as written records begin to be kept with the coming of Christianity.

The Early Historic Period

The centuries from 500 to 1000 AD are a blend of fact and legend, tangible and intangible evidence. Linguistic elements in place names and dedications point to a mix of ethnic groups in the population and wide contacts. Although origins and definitions can be disputed, there are clearly elements of Brittonic, (the indigenous Celtic akin to Welsh) as in Blantyre/Blaen-tir; Scottish Celt (Gaelic) as in Carphin/Carr-fion, and

English (Anglo-Saxon) as in Eddlewood /Edulf's wood.

Two fine monuments also reflect these different ethnic groupings. The first is a 'hog-back' grave marker at Dalserf, which is a typically Anglian or English gravemarker of this period, probably dating to 900-1000 AD. This is named after its shape, and is carved with a pattern of scales on the sides.

The second is the Netherton Cross, once standing on Hamilton Low Parks, and now in the grounds of Hamilton Parish Churchyard. This free standing slab is shaped as a cross and carved on all four sides with geometric, animal and figural design. Spirals and interlace are mixed with human and mythical figures, fish and animals. Its unusual mix of styles shows Viking as well as Celtic influence, and it is also believed to date to the 900s AD.

Early Celtic saints abound in place names and dedications – St. Ninian at Stonehouse, St. Patrick at Dalpatrick, St. Serf and St. Machan at Dalserf.

St. Kentigern, or Mungo, of Glasgow figures strongly, too, converting Rederech, the King of Strathclyde and Langoreth, his Queen, to Christianity in 568. Here at the royal hunting lodge or castle of Cadzow, Kentigern saved the Queen from the folly of giving a ring to a lover, through its miraculous return by a salmon, – a legend which forms part of the City of Glasgow's coat of arms.

1000-1700 AD

As we move into the medieval period, this area retains strong royal connections. David I and Alexander II signed a number of charters at Cadzow. These granted land to supporters, and David may have had a royal hunting lodge here. He may also have been responsible for planting the oak forest at Cadzow, parts of which are 800 years old. The site of the lodge is not proven, although claims have been made for the later ruined Cadzow Castle being on the earlier site.

The names of other landowners start to appear, like David Olifard, granted the lands of Bothwell, before they pass to Walter de Moravia (Moray) in 1242, and the Earls of Douglas in the 1360s. The former two are from immigrant families of Anglo-Norman origin rather than native landowners, and reflect the promotion of those loyal to the monarch. Another such may be Sir William the Fleming of 'Stanhus' or Stonehouse, found signing charters in the reign of Alexander II, around 1214, and another was definitely John Comyn, baron of Cadzow and claimant to the Scottish throne, murdered by Robert Bruce in 1306.

His lands, including Eddlewood, Machan (Dalserf) and the barony, were granted to one Walter fitzGilbert, known as de Hameldone. It is from this man that the Hamilton family and the current Dukedom descend. The family took the name Hamilton from 1375, but the estate name was changed in 1445 when Sir James Hamilton was created Lord Hamilton. This promotion followed the fall from power of the Douglases, and when Lord Hamilton married Princess Mary, daughter of James II, he was created 1st Earl of Arran as well. The family rose significantly in influence and prestige, and, reflecting this raised status, Lord James founded a collegiate church at Hamilton in 1450-51, a college at Glasgow University in 1460 (the first layman to found a college in Scotland) and, in 1475, had Hamilton raised to burgh status. It became a Royal Burgh in 1548.

The granting of lands by feudal charter created uniform administrative and legal structures across the country, as well as starting estate patterns which have influenced the development of communities in this area, and the lives of the population at every level. As estate management affected the physical lives of the people, so the development of religious structures created spiritual cohesion and patterns of social life.

The move from the Celtic to Roman Catholic church organisation between 1050 and 1200 gradually produced a network of parishes within dioceses run by bishops, which has been modified only slightly since. These parishes are Cadzow, or Hamilton, which originally included Dalserf (separated off after the Reformation), Blantyre, Bothwell (which included Shotts until after the Reformation) and Stonehouse. All the churches in this area were part of Glasgow Diocese, which included most of south and west Scotland.

Revenue from parish churches was often granted to larger religious houses, as happened at Hamilton, where David I granted it to Glasgow Cathedral. Individual landowners followed the national pattern of setting up religious communities of various forms. An early instance was the founding of Blantyre Priory by Patrick, Earl of Dunbar, between 1238 and 1249, and Hamilton Collegiate Church was a later example.

In 1560, however, the Reformation swept away the Roman Catholic church structure and theology, and Scotland's church became Protestant. While the physical structure of buildings and parish divisions persisted, the theology and organisation of the Reformed church was to take a further 130 years of bitter and often violent conflict to resolve and become

11

established by law.

The Reformation seems to have been accepted without great upheaval in this area. Most of the clergy such as William Chirnside, who had formerly been Provost of Bothwell Church, accepted the change. Chirnside became the Minister at Blantyre. One of the first appointments of a Minister to the reformed church was that of Robert Thomson, a friend of John Knox, who was appointed to Hamilton by the first ever General Assembly of the Church in Glasgow at Christmas, 1561. The parishes became a part of the new Hamilton Presbytery.

The power of the Hamiltons was a mixed blessing to the family and to the people of the area. Politics and religion are seldom far apart, and the Hamiltons were in the thick of both for most of this period.

The 1st Earl of Arran held significant power during the minority of James V, and gained the lands of Bothwell. The 2nd Earl was Governor of Scotland in the first two years of the infant Mary Queen of Scots's reign. His part in arranging Mary's marriage to the Dauphin of France gained him a French Dukedom (of Chatelherault), and he was leader of the Lords of the Congregation who carried the Reformation through Parliament in 1560.

But high profile involvement brings not only great rewards, but also great losses, as the balance of power and favour shift. Hamilton Castle was besieged in 1515 and, in 1565, the 2nd Earl was forced into exile after an unsuccessful rebellion against Mary. Changing allegiance, he again ended up on the losing side in 1568, when Mary rallied support from Hamilton and went to defeat at Langside before fleeing to England. These upheavals affected the area as well as the family, with opposing armies wasting the Hamilton properties and estate, notably in 1572 and 1579.

The ups and downs continued through the 1600s, with members of the family supporting different sides in the civil and religious struggles which swept Britain under Charles I, Cromwell, Charles II, and James VII (and II). The religious struggle was between a Presbyterian and an Episcopal system of church government, and supporters of the former were known as Covenanters from their support for the National Covenant of 1638. The west and south of Scotland were staunchly Covenanting, and suffered for it.

The widow of the 2nd Marquis, Lady Anna Cunninghame, was strongly Presbyterian, and is reputed to have ridden with pistols at the head of a troop of soldiers to prevent her son, the 3rd Marquis, landing

View of Hamilton, John Slezer, 1693

pro-Charles troops on the east coast. The 3rd Marquis was Charles's Commissioner to the General Assembly of 1638 and failed to prevent it abolishing Episcopacy. In 1649, he led an army into England to free Charles I, but was defeated at Preston, and executed. His brother, William, fought for Charles II at the Battle of Worcester, and died of wounds received there. During Cromwell's Commonwealth, the town of Hamilton had an English garrison and, in 1650, a surprise attack by a Covenanting force was beaten off at the battle of Hieton.

When Charles II was restored in 1660, repression of Covenanters intensified. All but one of the ministers in the Presbytery of Hamilton were evicted or 'outed' from their parishes for non-conformity, and many local people were outlawed or heavily fined.

In 1666, local men joined a general rebellion which was defeated at Rullion Green near Edinburgh. A memorial to four local men who were executed for taking part stands in the Parish churchyard. A second revolt began in 1679, when armed Covenanters defeated a company of dragoons under Graham of Claverhouse at Drumclog, near Strathaven. The Covenanting army grew, and camped on Hamilton Muir, but was defeated at the subsequent battle at Bothwell Bridge by the Duke of Monmouth's army.

Duchess Anne is said to have saved many Covenanters from capture by asking the Duke not to send troops into her estate in case they disturbed the game, but many prisoners were taken and executions followed. Peace did not come until 1690 when William and Mary established the Presbyterian church in Scotland by law. Apart from the many memorials erected in the area to commemorate those who suffered, the most lasting outcome for this area was the founding in 1689 of what would become the Cameronians (Scottish Rifles) Regiment, disbanded in 1968.

1700-Present

As the century turned, a view of the area would show little difference from previous centuries, but its character was beginning to alter at an ever increasing speed, until its former shape is in many places almost undetectable.

Hamilton was a small town spreading from the Palace up the slope from Netherton to Hieton, and the parish church was still the old Collegiate Church close to the Palace which had been used since the Reformation. No other settlement in the area came close to it in size,

14

with Bothwell, Blantyre, Uddingston, Dalserf, Larkhall and Stonehouse being small villages in a predominantly agricultural landscape. Industry was low key, and served mostly the local market, whether coalmining, weaving, tanning or brewing.

By the mid 1700s, a change was brewing and between 1790 and 1830, the district population nearly trebled from 8,924 to 24,954. Initially, this was due to weaving, which became a major industry throughout the area. The Duchess Anne and her grandson, the 5th Duke, had completed an ambitious plan to lay out the Estate to a 'Great Design' reflecting their wealth and position, and that included the encouragement of industry to fund the change. Duchess Anne established a wool weaving factory in Hamilton, and Duchess Elizabeth founded a school for twelve girls and a mistress to encourage the production of lace. At that time the Misses Leslie at Uddingston were producing thread from locally grown flax which received national acclaim.

Originally weaving was a home based cottage industry, but the development of water powered mills allowed the area to benefit from the industrial revolution and increased trade with America. Large cotton mills were constructed on the Clyde, most famously at New Lanark, but also at Blantyre in the 1780s. Domestic work continued into the 1800s although the balance shifted from handloom weaving to women's work of tambour lace making. Weaving played a major part in virtually all the communities of the area – Hamilton, Larkhall, Stonehouse, Blantyre, Bothwell and Uddingston. As the century progressed, the industry declined in all areas, beaten by the increased competition of the large mills.

Coal had been exploited for centuries, possibly since the monks of Lesmahagow in the 1300s, and certainly in the surface deposits and easily reached horizontal and shallow beds from the 1600s, with coal being extracted for Hamilton Palace from drift mines at Quarter. The Old Statistical Accounts of the area in the 1790s record four sources in use in Bothwell parish, and the Minister at Stonehouse laments the under use of the resource in his area, although plenty is available from the four mines in the Dalserf area.

It was not, however, until the mid 1800s, with technology allowing deep mining and improved transport links from the railways, that this became a major factor in the life and character of the area. Over a hundred mines were opened in the boom times between 1860 and 1920, and mines became the major employer. Iron ore has also been mined, and the availability of coal and iron encouraged the growth of industrial steel production locally. Both coal and steel were exported via Glasgow across the globe.

All this changed after the First World War as demand slumped and the best seams were worked out. Many mines closed in the 1920s and 1930s, leaving a changed physical landscape from the workings and spoil, and a changed population from the large scale immigration into the area that the employment boom encouraged. This turned a primarily agricultural and rural landscape into one heavily dominated at the north of the district by industrial and urban sprawl, and has broadened and enriched the social mix and life of the community, even though this change has also brought its tensions.

The villages of Bothwell, Blantyre, Uddingston and Larkhall mushroomed, forming in the north end of the district an almost continuous blanket of housing and industry. The expansion of the road and rail network allowed for commuting, and assisted this growth. From the turn of the century, railway expansion also encouraged a boom in commercial fruit growing along the Clyde valley, which lasted until after the Second World War. Today the closeness of the M74 and the motorway network still make this an attractive area, less than twenty minutes from Glasgow city centre.

As the century has progressed, industry has diversified. As the mines closed down steel expanded with the creation of the Ravenscraig-Dalzell-Gartcosh complex in the 1950/60s across the Clyde. Until its gradual closure in the 1990s, this provided jobs for much of Lanarkshire.

Now new industrial estates are being established jointly through the District Council, Lanarkshire Development Agency and Strathclyde Regional Council with assistance from central government and European funds for smaller scale, lighter industries more suited to today's markets. There has been a significant growth in the service industry base, which accounts for around 35% of local employment, while there are still continuing international success stories, such as Tunnock's of Uddingston.

Derelict industrial landscapes are being reclaimed for redevelopment and landscaping to create a better environment and quality of life for the area. There have been extensive improvements to housing and leisure facilities in the past twenty years, thanks to the respective local Councils. These have included the three Civic Centres at Hillhouse, Whitehill and Fairhill, sports centres at Larkhall and Blantyre and sports barns

16

around the District.

William Adam's restored Lodges at Chatelherault, built in the 1730s for the 5th Duke, were opened with a Visitor Centre to the public in 1987, at the centre of a 550 acre country park with ten miles of paths through forest and the Avon Gorge. These, along with the District Museum and Cameronians (Scottish Rifles) Regimental Museum, are being redeveloped in 1995-1996. The new Water Palace opened in Hamilton in 1995.

In the 1960s, Hamilton town centre was substantially rebuilt to create a shopping focus for the town and surrounding area. Now the Hamilton Ahead Project, launched in 1994, is beginning an exciting initiative to extend and revitalise the town centre in line with present needs, and to link housing, offices, shopping and leisure in such a way as to sustain Hamilton's role as one of Scotland's premier towns. The complex will involve new building and a town square on Hamilton Low Parks and Palace grounds.

As we look to South Lanarkshire, we take with us a history and heritage of which we can be proud, and on whose solid achievements a positive future is already being built.

HAMILTON

Joyce J. R. Brown

"It is sometimes said, not without a measure of truth, that there are but two classes of people in Hamilton – Hamiltonians and incomers. Of the distinction which attaches to him, the Hamiltonian is never in any doubt". So wrote the Reverend John Fraser when compiling the Third Statistical Account in 1954.

Officially, there were no Hamiltonians until 1445, for it was in that year that the burgeoning town was granted the name of Hamilton, in honour of Sir James Hamilton of Cadzow.

Cadzow, as the area was previously known, had become a royal barony under David I. The fact that both David I and Alexander II issued charters "apud Cadihou" (at Cadzow) would suggest that there was a royal residence in the area from at least 1139. There was also a church, which David I granted to the church and bishops of Glasgow in 1150.

The probable site of the early 'toun' of Cadzow was the low ground by the River Clyde, where a motte, or artificial mound, may be all that remains of an early castle. Under the feudal system, castles were key factors in establishing stable government, and were natural focal points for settlements.

Close to the motte was the tenth century Netherton Cross, which appears to be of religious significance, and is further evidence of settlement in this area.

In 1315, Robert the Bruce gifted the barony of Cadzow to Walter fitzGilbert de Hameldone (Hamilton), as a reward for transferring his allegiance to the Bruce after the battle of Bannockburn. The Hamiltons probably originated in Northumbria, but had settled in Scotland by 1296, when Walter fitzGilbert appeared on the Homage Roll of Lanarkshire lairds.

In 1445, his descendant, Sir James Hamilton, was made a lord of parliament, and his lands were created a "true, free and united" lordship, to be known as Hamilton. It would appear, however, that the name Hamilton was already in popular use, as an English state paper of 1413 refers to the town by that name.

In 1450-51, in keeping with his elevated status, Lord Hamilton petitioned the Pope for permission to erect a collegiate church in the town. A provost and eight chaplains were appointed, and were each given a manse, garden and glebe (portion of land). The church, which later acted as the parish church, was sited to the east of the town, close to the Hamilton family residence, called 'The Orchard'.

The new church was a very impressive building, consisting of a choir, two cross aisles and a steeple, all built of polished stone and highly ornamented. Mounted on various parts of the building were coats of arms, showing the marriage connections of the Hamilton family. The most important of these was the Hamilton arms combined with the royal arms, marking the marriage of Lord Hamilton's son to Princess Mary, sister of King James III.

The site chosen for the new church reveals that the town had by now spread south to higher ground near the Cadzow Burn, perhaps to avoid regular flooding by the Clyde. The new area was known as the Hietoun, and was connected to the earlier settlement, the Netherton, by a lane called Netherton Wynd.

In 1456, Hamilton was granted the status of a burgh of barony by charter from Lord Hamilton. This gave the town certain trading privileges, including the holding of fairs and weekly markets, but government was under the control of Lord Hamilton, the burgh superior.

We are given a brief glimpse of the fifteenth century burgh in a charter of 1475, by which Lord Hamilton grants to the community and bailies a bakehouse, a common green, and a common muir, as pasturage for the horses of travellers and townspeople. In return, the burgh was to pay a toll of 13s-4d annually, to be put towards the cost of maintaining a lamp in the church, for the salvation of the souls of Lord Hamilton, his predecessors and successors "and of all faithful dead".

The Hamilton family reached the peak of their political power during the reign of Mary, Queen of Scots, when James Hamilton, 2nd Earl of Arran, was appointed Governor of Scotland. At this time, the town was granted a royal charter, elevating it to royal burgh status. It now had the right to be protected by a wall, to elect its own town council and magistrates, and the exclusive right to trade within the surrounding area. Only royal burghs were allowed to trade overseas or to sell foreign imports, such as fine cloth, wax or French wine, making this a particularly lucrative privilege for a town.

In return for these privileges, the sovereign expected the loyalty of the inhabitants, particularly in the form of military assistance when necessary. Royal burghs also paid a 'cess' or tax, which was calculated proportionately to each burgh's income from trade, tolls and customs dues. It would appear that Hamilton was a small and relatively undeveloped burgh at this time, since it paid only 20 crowns in tax, in comparison to 60 crowns from Stirling and 180 crowns from Perth.

The Hamiltons' political power may have brought elevated status to the town, but their key role in the dramatic events of Mary's reign also brought the town more than its fair share of troubles. It was to Hamilton that Mary came after her escape from Lochleven, before being forced to flee to England after her defeat at Langside. In the following years, Mary's enemies took their revenge on her supporters. In 1570, Regent Moray was murdered by a member of the Hamilton family, James Hamilton of Bothwellhaugh, and, in an English punitive expedition, Hamilton castle was attacked with cannon, and "the toun and palice of Hamilton therewith burnt and demolished".

In 1591, Lord John Hamilton began building a new Palace, possibly on the site of the old one, close to the growing burgh. The town also seems to have recovered from former ravages and, in 1599, was chosen as the repository of the new register of sasines (charters of land ownership) for Lanarkshire.

However, the seventeenth century brought further troubles, when the town became a stronghold of the Covenanting movement. In 1650, Oliver Cromwell, who himself lodged in the King's Head Inn in the Hietoun, sent General Lambert to subdue the west of Scotland. Lambert took up position in Hamilton and there clashed with 1,500 Covenanters from Ayrshire. The Covenanters, despite capturing Lambert at one stage, were routed in the battle of the Hietoun.

The Hamilton family did not come through this troubled period unscathed. James, 3rd Marquis of Hamilton, was a close friend of Charles I and acted as his mediator in Scotland. He was rewarded with a dukedom, but, six years later, was executed by the Parliamentarians. His brother, the 2nd Duke, died fighting for the royalist cause, and was succeeded by his niece, Anne. Duchess Anne found herself facing financial ruin, as the Hamilton estates had been confiscated and handed over to various officers in Cromwell's army. After the restoration of Charles II in 1660, Duchess Anne and Duke William returned to the Palace, and soon began their 'Great Design' for the remodelling of the building and landscaping of the grounds.

This 'Great Design' was responsible for yet another shift in the town's location. The landscaping of the Palace grounds necessitated the full-scale evacuation and demolition of much of the old town. The Grammar School, which had existed since at least 1588, was replaced by a fine new schoolhouse on high ground to the south-west. Nearby, Duchess Anne built a new hospital, or almshouse, for eight poor men, in place of the hospital founded by the 2nd Marquis of Hamilton in 1615.

This process was continued by Duchess Anne's grandson, the 5th Duke of Hamilton, who demolished the collegiate church, and provided the town with a new parish church, designed by William Adam around 1732.

It would appear that the town had not been making use of all the privileges of a royal burgh, and, in 1670, it had been declared to be a burgh of regality, under the authority of Duchess Anne. She and her successors had the right to appoint the town clerk and two bailies, or magistrates, from a shortleet of six drawn up by the Town Council.

Burgh records give a fascinating insight into town life in the early eighteenth century. Gates, known as ports, controlled access to the burgh and allowed tolls to be collected on market goods. Hamilton had four main gates – the East Port, the Castle wynd Port, the Muir-wynd Port and the Netherton-wynd Port, but there are later references to a Miln Port.

The principal street was the High Street, running up in front of the Palace to the junction with Castle Wynd and Muir Wynd. Here sat the most important building in the burgh – the tolbooth, which acted as council chamber, court house and jail. Dating from 1642, it had an impressive steeple, in which the Town Council fitted a clock in 1656 at a cost of £314-13s-8d. Four years later, a further £45 was spent on a new tolbooth bell, weighing 8 stones 8 lbs. In 1666, Jon Pate, town officer, was paid the annual salary of £30 "for keeping of the clock and ringing the bell". On the ground floor of the tolbooth there were three booths, or shops, which were let annually, providing extra income for the burgh revenues.

Outside the tolbooth were the burgh stocks, where wrongdoers were padlocked by the ankles. In 1670, James Hamilton, a Hamilton merchant, was "to be brought publicly to the market cross, and be laid in the stocks" for striking his parents and uttering "vile and unchristian expressions".

Nearby stood the mercat cross, a symbol of the town's trading rights, and a focus for public events, from markets to floggings. Weekly markets were originally held on Saturdays and Sundays but, in 1661, Duchess Anne obtained an Act of Parliament changing the Saturday market to Friday. The Saturday market had proved inconvenient, in that "the people resorting to it are much occasioned in their return homeward to be late in the night, and sometime to encroach on the Lord's day next ensuing, and so scandalous to God's worship".

At the same time, the number of annual fairs was increased from two to four. The original fairs were held on St. Lawrence's day (August) and St. Martin's day (November), but there was now said to be need of a fair "in the beginning of the springtime when the throng of the labour to the ground is greatest, and so requiring a conveniency of buying and selling workhorses for ploughing and harrowing". Similarly, a fair was needed at Whitsunday (June) to allow the country people an opportunity of selling goods before their rent was due.

Near to the market place was the tron, or public weighing machine, where market goods were checked before being sold. The first tron may have dated from 1595, but was renewed in 1661, and again in 1712. By 1774, it was said to be "entirely decayed and about falling down" and this time, in order "to beautify the street", it was moved to the "east gable of Mr. Boyse's large tenement".

Running north from the High Street was Muir Wynd, leading to the common muir, where the townspeople pastured their cows and horses. Until the 1830s, Muir Wynd formed the main highway through the town, and at the top was Gallowshill, the place of public execution. Branching off Muir Wynd, where it joined the rough road to Bothwell, was a small footpath through the whins. In 1736, this track was 'causeyed' for road passengers, and later formed the basis of Almada Street and Burnbank Road.

South of the High Street was Castle Wynd, leading to Townhead, Broken Cross, where the Quakers held their meetings, and Quarry Loan. The Donaghadee quarry was in existence by 1637 but, as yet, there were very few houses in this area.

One of the newest streets was School Wynd, or New Wynd, leading to the Grammar School, erected by Duchess Anne in 1714. Beyond this, a path, later known as Kirk Road, and, more recently, as Church Street, led to the new parish church. This church was erected on the site of the horse and cow market at the annual Martinmas fair. The Town Council, realising that the remainder of the ground would "be taken up with houses which the townspeople will probably build for the conveniency of being near the church", moved the horse market to the head of Castle Wynd. The first houses were built in Kirk Road in 1751.

Although public buildings like the church, school, tolbooth and almshouse were built of stone, most houses in the burgh were constructed of timber, with thatched or turfed roofs. Fire was a constant danger. In 1740, the Town Council, "considering that the town of Hamilton consists

Top Cross, Quarry Street and the Old Town Hall

Former Tolbooth, Old Cross c 1880

generally of thatched houses and that frequent accident fires happen on account of the foulness of vents" ordered all chimneys to be swept three times a year. Despite this, in 1744, a terrible fire raged through Barric's Close for eight days, and destroyed much property in the town. Four years later, the town's first "water engine for extinguishing fires" was purchased in Edinburgh for £18.

Most houses had by now been removed from the vicinity of the Palace, but the old Netherton Wynd still led down to that area. Running south from there was the Langloan, which gave access to the Clyde ferry. Until the first Clyde bridge was built in 1780, the ferry was the only means of crossing the river. Unusually, there were two boats maintained at the quay – a "meikle" (large) boat for cattle and carriages, and a "little" boat for foot passengers. Fares ranged from a halfpenny for foot passengers to two shillings for a coach with six horses.

The improvement of transport links became increasingly important in the eighteenth century. The town's craftsmen, who had originally supplied goods purely for local needs, were now manufacturing goods for much wider markets. Duchess Anne had gifted a woollen manufactory to the town in 1706 and, by the 1750s, a flourishing lacemaking industry had developed. In 1725, the most numerous craftsmen were the shoemakers and the weavers. By 1790, the number of weavers' looms in the parish had risen from 250 to 450. Glasgow was the principal market for cotton goods but, until the 1750s, most goods had to be transported by packhorse, since the roads were little more than rough tracks. The introduction of the Turnpike System in 1750 allowed Turnpike Trusts to build and maintain roads on the income derived from tolls payable by all road users.

One of the first turnpike roads in the area was the Edinburgh to Ayr highway, which was constructed in 1773. Quarry Street developed as part of this highway and, in 1830, the Top Cross was formed when two new streets – Duke Street and Brandon Street – joined Quarry Street at the site of the former horse and cow market.

The most radical change in Hamilton was the construction of Thomas Telford's new Glasgow to Carlisle highway. The previous route south, via Muir Wynd, had long been recognised as a difficult road for coaches, and many accidents occurred at the notorious 'devil's elbow', close to the tolbooth. To avoid this route, the new highway required the construction of a road and bridge across the Cadzow Burn. The new road – Cadzow Street – was authorised by parliament in 1819, and completed around 1835. The Duke of Hamilton provided most of the money for Cadzow

Bridge, which, at 60 feet high and with a span of 180 feet, was the most expensive element of the street. Telford's Bridge over the River Avon was built in 1825 as part of the same highway.

With Cadzow Street as the main highway, the focus moved upwards from the old town. Banks, houses and shops "of elegant appearance" opened along the street, which soon became the commercial heart of the town. The area around Castle Wynd was now referred to as 'the old town', a description which is still applied today.

By this time, the population of Hamilton had doubled to 7,500, and there were 1,291 weaving looms in the town. Rows of weavers' cottages had formed new streets, such as Low Patrick Street, Almada Street and Saffronhall Lane. A room and kitchen with a four-loom weaving shop could be rented for around £5 per annum, at a time when wages were 6d. (2½p) to 1s 6d. (7½p) per day.

The expansion of the town was partly due to the establishment of a suburban railway terminus near Peacock Cross. The Hamilton Directory of 1855 stated that "the railway to Glasgow – half an hour's ride – is making Hamilton a genteel suburb of that great city, what Richmond on the Thames is to London". The appearance of commuting Glasgow merchants, attracted by "the woodlands and the pure air", led landowners to draw up extensive feuing schemes for their estates. The former lands of Auchingramont were laid out in crescents, streets and terraces, and Mr. Clark of Hollandbush was said to be "prepared to feu the whole for villas". Villas in the town were said to be of "comfortable simplicity and generally tasteful character". Auchingramont Road, Park Road, Clydesdale Street and Union Street all came into existence in this period.

The opening of the Caledonian Central Railway station in 1876 led to the further development of Quarry Street, which soon rivalled Cadzow Street as the principal shopping area of the town. In 1879, it was said that "ere long this neighbourhood will become the centre of the burgh".

Despite the relentless expansion, it was possible for one writer to say that "here was still an oasis where the eye could wander over undulating fields and tree-clad heights yet untouched by the indomitable mercantile spirit which has converted the Clyde valley into a teeming hive of industry".

This all changed with the mining boom between 1870 and 1920. By 1874, there were twenty two collieries in Hamilton parish, many of them situated within the town. The 1879 Hamilton Directory took a pessimistic view, stating that "the amenity of the district has to be sacrificed for the good of the country at large. Railways have cut it up in all directions; its romantic rocks serve but for piers to the unromantic girder bridge; and over the trees rises the coalpit head-gear, with its attendant chimney stalk, darkening the air with smoke and smudge".

By 1881, the population had trebled to over 26,000, with the influx of immigrants from all over Scotland, England, and especially Ireland. Miners' rows, such as those at Earnock, Cadzow, and Greenfield, were speedily erected around the collieries. The former villages of Burnbank and Low-waters grew into extensive suburbs, and were incorporated into the burgh in 1878.

The speed and scale of these industrial developments left little scope for good town planning, and the rapidly increasing population put a strain on existing amenities such as water supply, sanitation, education and poor relief.

Water was collected at public wells, which were often contaminated with sewage. Household waste was deposited in middens in front of every house. Waterborne diseases, such as cholera and typhoid, were rife, and poverty was concentrated in the areas hit by trade recessions.

The Hamilton Directory of 1855 published a list of "Things Wanted", which included water pipes and a water closet in every house, better sewers and drainage, a poorhouse, a fever hospital and the removal of the old town.

Hamilton got a piped water supply in 1857, a Combination Poorhouse in 1867, a fever hospital in 1879, and sewage works in 1907. In addition, a public gas supply had been introduced in 1831, to be followed by electricity works in 1903. By the early twentieth century, reform had spread through most aspects of town life, except for housing.

In 1914, in response to a proposal to carry out an improvement scheme in Low Waters, a Medical Inspector reported on housing conditions in the town. On a visit to New Wynd, he found a "house of one dark room with roof sagging very badly. Occupied by parents and two children. No water in. No water-closet". In Quarry Street he described a "house entered from back-yard under stair. This backyard is very dirty. Domestic washing going on here while an old man lay in bed wheezing with bronchitis". Unfortunately, the conditions were typical of the properties visited.

Hamilton Town Council swiftly began a programme of slum demolition, which resulted in the building of over 1,000 municipally owned houses in areas such as Glenlee, Low Waters and the old town. The Duke of Hamilton gifted a number of obsolete properties in the old town, thereby allowing the area to be redeveloped more quickly. The Duke wished the scheme to be carried out "with due regard to providing the necessary housing for the population to be displaced and with the least possible hardship to the poorer classes of tenants".

Although a further 1,176 municipal houses were built between 1920 and 1930, the problems remained acute. Under the Housing (Scotland) Act of 1935, overcrowding was defined for the first time and became an offence. A survey of 1936 revealed that overcrowding in Hamilton ran at 39%, 10% higher than Glasgow, and only exceeded by four other towns in Scotland.

Not surprisingly, the number of local authority houses built in Hamilton increased to 3,000 in the decade between 1930 and 1940. The three main areas developed were Udston, Fairhill and Whitehill.

After the Second World War, demands for housing increased. People wanted something better than the room and kitchen which was typical of over 40% of Scotland's housing. To fulfill the demand in the short-term, Hamilton built 233 temporary homes or 'prefabs'. The long-term answer was a new type of housing scheme at Hillhouse, where 1,300 houses were erected between 1952 and 1962. This scheme was based on the same principle as new towns like East Kilbride, and was developed as a complete neighbourhood unit, with all the amenities considered necessary for the wellbeing of the community.

With the end of the mining boom, and the lack of alternative employment, Hamilton had been declared a 'distressed area' in 1931. However, a survey carried out in 1948 showed that the face of Hamilton had changed yet again. There were now large numbers of people engaged in public administration and the professions, emphasising Hamilton's position as the administrative centre of Lanarkshire. Of the 16,449 inhabitants in employment, over half worked elsewhere, suggesting that Hamilton had become, to a large extent, a dormitory town for Glasgow and other business centres. This was to remain the pattern for the next fifty years.

More recently, recession and the decline of traditional industries have had a major impact on the local economy. As a result, industrial and commercial development is a priority for the town, but this is balanced with a new environmental awareness and an appreciation of our heritage. Hamilton may be conscious of its heritage as "an old ducal, garrison and county town", but it nevertheless looks forward and moves with the times, as it has had to do all through its history. Conservation is not about the past, it is about the future.

A DESCRIPTION OF HAMILTON

There is ample elbow room and ventilation. Every man may cultivate his cabbage or smoke his cigar under his own apple tree in peace and quiet. The houses are sprinkled over area enough for a large city. There is plenty of room to grow. Like the young towns in the far west, we have carved out an ambitious outline to fill up at leisure; but ample room and rations is the cry of the day.

Brown's Hamilton Directory, 1855

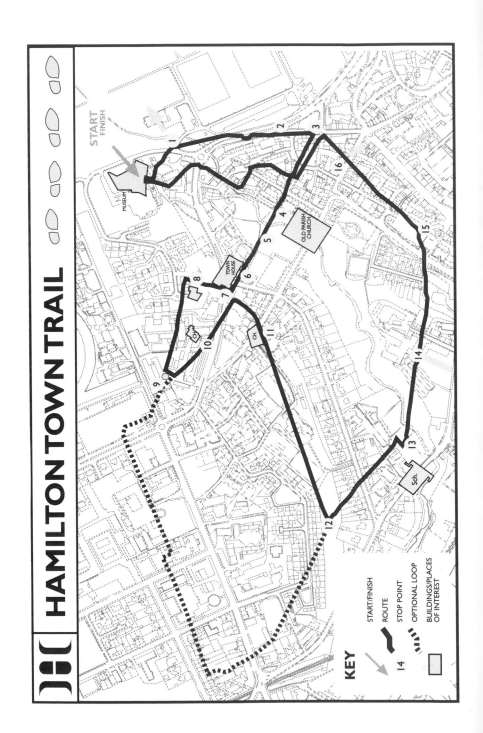

HAMILTON TOWN TRAIL

KEY

START/FINISH

ROUTE

STOP POINT

14

OPTIONAL LOOP

BUILDINGS/PLACES
OF INTEREST

START
FINISH

MUSEUM

OLD PARISH
CHURCH

TOWN
HOUSE

CH.

Sch.

A WALK AROUND HAMILTON

William Wallace

Introduction

Hamilton's best architecture was designed in the Victorian era, a time when there were many stonemasons of great skill and when suitable sandstone was available from local quarries. Before the end of the nineteenth century, however, there is evidence that stone was being brought in from Dumfriesshire, Renfrewshire and Stirlingshire. Sadly, many of the old buildings had to be demolished, either because of dereliction or subsidence caused by mining. Casualties have included Hamilton Palace and the old Gaol and Tolbooth.

In the late nineteenth century, Hamilton produced several architects of distinction, many of whose buildings are included in this walk – Alexander Cullen, his son, also Alexander, and Gavin Paterson. Alexander Cullen was born in 1857, and was apprenticed to a Motherwell mason, before starting a business of his own. He later went to Glasgow University to train as an architect. One of his commissions was work on Ross House in 1899, and, in 1902, firmly established in Brandon Chambers, he took on James Lochhead and William Brown as partners. Cullen died in 1911, but his company continues to this day. Gavin Paterson was in practice in Hamilton by 1894, and although he died in 1934, the business continued until the 1980s.

Architectural features abound above eye-level – watch out for all of them, particularly weather vanes and ornamental features on roofs. While road safety and care must always be given the utmost priority, there are times, too, when it is possible to look down at one's feet! Perhaps, then, we can see man-holes and gratings which often carry the name of the foundry where they were forged. Look out, too, for wrought iron gates. The iron work at Church Street above the Parish Church gate is particularly fine. So, too, are the railings at Hamilton College which came originally from Hamilton Palace and were made in 1834. Almost opposite, in the public park in Bothwell Road, is the Bandstand made at the Saracen foundry in Glasgow and erected in 1912. The Palace railings and the Bandstand are both part of the list of buildings of architectural or historic interest, a copy of which can be seen in the Hamilton Reference Library.

Finally, a feature to be looked for is the broad arrow or benchmark ^, carved on walls at very wide intervals. This represents the surveyor's mark made when carrying out the Royal Ordnance Survey.

The Walk

The Walk around Hamilton is between one and two miles long, dependent on which option you choose, and lasts from one and a half to two hours. It is all along pavements, with some gentle inclines. Instructions as to each stage of the walk are given in italics. The numbered stop points on the map are shown in brackets.

Start from the pavement outside Hamilton Museum which was built in 1696 as the home of David Crawford, Secretary to the Duchess Anne. It is likely to have been designed by James Smith of Edinburgh who was responsible for the alterations to Hamilton Palace carried out at that time. There are records that show it was pillaged by a mob in December, 1745, when the Jacobite army arrived in Hamilton. In the latter part of that century, it served as an inn and here such famous travellers as Dr Johnson and William Wordsworth were entertained. The Hamilton Arms, as it was known, ceased to be an inn in the 1830s at which time the building was used as offices by the Duke's Chamberlain. It continued to be used for this function until it was acquired by Hamilton Town Council and converted into a museum, which opened in 1967.

Cross at the roundabout to the town side of Castle Street, note Cadzow Burn, and pause to look back at the Low Parks (1).

The pink sandstone building set back from the road was designed by William Burn of Edinburgh, and erected in 1832 as the Duke's Riding School.

Look further right and back to see the Mausoleum built for Duke Alexander the 10th and completed in 1856. Immediately to your right, across the road, was the Old Cross of Hamilton where the ancient Tolbooth and Gaol stood. The clock tower of the Tolbooth was deliberately blown up in 1953! Beyond it stood Hamilton Palace, the grandest stately home of its time in Scotland, demolished in the 1920s and 1930s following subsidence from mining.

Our walk now takes us up Castle Street, the old Castle Wynd created in the days when Hamilton Palace was known as Hamilton Castle. Here, on the left corner with Edinburgh Road, is the building which served as the former office of the Royal Bank of Scotland (2).

Going on up from there to the Bottom Cross we (3) come to Douglas Chambers on the left corner, at the entrance to Keith Street, probably named after Provost Keith who was instrumental in its creation. Keith Street had to be made up when electric trams first came along in 1903, to allow the trams, which could not manage the sharp turn from Castle Street, to come in from Motherwell. Douglas Chambers, built in 1903 as a three storey commercial building, was designed by Alexander Cullen, as were Nos. 1-9 Keith Street. Cullen was also responsible for the church built for the Methodists in 1908 which is now the Salvation Army Temple, further down Keith Street on the right.

Next to Douglas Chambers, at No.11, is the Vogue Bingo Hall, opened in 1921 as the La Scala cinema. The prominent red sandstone building, No.2 Keith Street, on the corner with Townhead Street, contains a clock which was gifted to the town in 1925 by the Trustees of the late Thomas McGill, a sweet manufacturer.

Moving right into Cadzow Street, on the right corner is a finely designed red sandstone building by the architect Gavin Paterson, who also used it as his offices. These were the premises of the Commercial Bank of Scotland and were erected in 1899. Next to the building are Nos.8-42 Cadzow Street, probably dating from the later 1830s or 1840s, when much of the Street was erected. Cadzow Street takes its name from the earliest recorded name for the district.

Directly opposite Church Street, you will see the Old Parish Church (4), built by William Adam in 1734, when the Collegiate Church was demolished to allow for the Palace to expand. The churchyard has several fine memorials in it, including the Netherton Cross and Covenanters' stones, and can be entered through the gate at the top end. Follow Cadzow Lane into Leechlee Road and round into Strathmore Road to gain access.

On your right as you face the Parish Church from Cadzow Street are interesting blocks at No.1 Church Street on the corner, and going up to Nos.77-93 Cadzow Street, beyond to the right. This is known as Cadzow Buildings and was erected in three stages between 1847 and 1863 by the controversial Councillor John Tainsh, who was threatened with bankruptcy and jail in the 1870s.

Back on the right side of Cadzow Street heading towards the bridge is No.88, the former office of the Commercial Bank which was acquired by James Keith, a grocer at No.86. It was the Keith family who built the handsome red sandstone property at No.94, at the same time as Cadzow Bridge was widened in 1901, when a double tram track was laid.

On the left side of Cadzow Street, before the bridge you can see a set of wrought iron railings commemorating the accession to the throne of Queen Elizabeth II, following the death of King George VI in 1952. The railings include the Hamilton coat of arms (5).

Cadzow Bridge was originally built in 1835. A plaque was erected in the middle of the bridge, on the right side, by the Hamilton Civic

North British Railway Station, Hamilton

MUNICIPAL BUILDINGS AND PUBLIC LIBRARY, HAMILTON. A-6085

Cadzow Street, Library and Town House

35

Society. This commemorates the battle of the Hieton fought near here on 1st December, 1650. Cromwell had established a garrison in Hamilton at that time and they were surprised by a force of Covenanters. Cromwell's men, however, regrouped and drove the Covenanters out with heavy losses. Below, by the bank of Cadzow Burn, is Hamilton's Common Green, exchanged in 1695 for one that stood near Hamilton Palace. The gift of the Green and the Parish Church were part of the general move of the town away from the Low Parks area to allow for the laying out of the Great Design for the Hamilton Estate, and the expansion of the Palace.

Go across the bridge and on the right are the Municipal Buildings or Town House, of which Hamiltonians can be very proud (6). The first section, the Library, was opened by the philanthropist, Andrew Carnegie, who had donated a substantial sum to finance its construction. The architect, Alexander Cullen, designed the Library in 1907, and his company, Cullen, Lochhead and Brown were responsible for the design of the remainder of the building which was opened by His Majesty, King George V, in 1914.

On the opposite (left) side at 105 Cadzow Street sits the building erected as offices by the legal firm of T. J. & W. A. Dykes. It also served as premises for the Royal Bank of Scotland for a number of years. This handsome structure dates from 1871.

Beyond here at No.113 is another distinguished building which dates from 1850 and was designed by William Spence of Glasgow. Originally built for the Western Bank, it was taken over by the Bank of Scotland in 1857.

On the corner beyond the Bank of Scotland, you can now see No.115 Cadzow Street, which was built in 1931 as new premises for the British Linen Bank which, until then, operated at No.4 Auchingramont Road. The architect for this building was Alexander Cullen II. One of the finest properties in the town sits opposite on the right at No.104. This is the Hamilton Kilwinning Masonic Lodge, No.7, built of local Earnock stone, which is a masterpiece design of Alexander Cullen and dates from 1904. It stretches round the corner and into Lower Auchingramont Road, where the entrance to the Town Hall, built in 1928, can also be viewed (7).

Continue downhill to the corner of Muir Street and Auchingramont Road to see Smellie's Auction Market originally erected as the Relief Church in 1776 (8). This date can still be seen on a little round window on the Muir Street side of the building. The only other building of interest on Muir Street is downhill from Lower Auchingramont Road – an eighteenth century dwelling called Wharrie House. It was called after Dr

36

Thomas Wharrie who was born in 1755.

Turning left up Muir Street hill, below the back of St Mary's Church, is the old eighteenth century Hamilton Manse.

The junction of Cadzow Street and Muir Street is marked by the Watson Fountain, a gift from John Watson, coal master of Earnock (9). It dates from 1893. Its architect was Gavin Paterson of Hamilton and the sculptures were by Killock Brown of Glasgow. Mrs Watson is supposed to have posed for the figure of "mining" which is in the centre.

At this point there are two options. Either the walk can be extended into a larger loop up to Almada Street, Peacock Cross, and down Union Street to rejoin the main walk at the junction with Auchingramont Road, or you can turn left back into Cadzow Street.

The Extended Walk

The loop will take you on uphill past a Lodge for Hamilton Palace on the right at the roundabout.

Turn left into Almada Street to see Bell College built on the site of the Cavalry Barracks (established during the Napoleonic Wars, and which continued as a local barracks for the Cameronians and other troops in transit until 1967), and the new Water Palace opened in 1995 to replace the old Hamilton Baths which can be seen beyond. Built in 1907, the baths are one of the oldest surviving municipal bath buildings in Scotland. On the right is the Sheriff Court, opened here in 1835 and, as well as serving Town and Country for this purpose, it was also the administrative headquarters of the Burgh. David Hamilton of Glasgow, the architect who also worked at Hamilton Palace, was responsible for its design.

Beyond the Sheriff Court are the County Buildings, designed by D G Bannerman in the style of the United Nations Building in New York. The building stands sixteen storeys tall and was opened by Her Majesty, Queen Elizabeth, the Queen Mother, in 1964. A fine Victorian cottage, "Douglasdale", stands at the corner of Almada Street and Douglas Street. There is an old milestone incorporated in its boundary wall, a single squared block towards the gable wall of 130 Almada Street, which reads "Glasgow 10 Hamilton 1". Looking right down Douglas Street, the tall brick chimney of the former Clyde Colliery can be seen.

Continue on till Peacock Cross is reached and, on the opposite corner of Wellhall Road and Burnbank Road, there is the red sandstone building erected in 1895 as the Peacock Bar. Some doubt exists as to the original date of the whole property. Peacock is a family name.

Turn left into Union Street built in 1841 by the Cambuslang Road Trustees as part of the Carlisle/Glasgow highway. The street has some very fine old houses, but the upper part of the street had to be raised prior to the opening of the North British Railway Station at Cadzow Street in 1874. Consequently, on the right, Cadzow Cottage or Cadzowburn (opposite the playpark) as it was later called, is below the present level of the street. So, too, is Linnholm which stands near to the highway.

Proceed down Union Street to join the shorter walk at the corner of Auchingramont Road and Union Street.

The Shorter Walk

Turning left along Cadzow Street. On the right a lane leads uphill. This is Windmill Road which takes its name from the site of the town windmill built in 1743. On the left is the Roman Catholic Church of St Mary, built in a Gothic style and similar to St Joseph's in Kilmarnock. It was erected in 1846 and the Chapel House (No.118a) is of similar date (10).

Muirbrow Chambers at No.118, built of red sandstone, is a design of Gavin Paterson dated 1913. No.116 is the former offices of the Lanarkshire Miners' Union, a Cullen building of 1907. Note the carved handshake above the door. Nos.108-112 are dated 1905 and were designed by Cullen or his partnership. No.114, built of yellow sandstone, is the old Silverwells House which dates from the 1840s.

Turn right into Auchingramont Road to see an imposing street of Victorian villas. Originally the driveway to the now demolished Auchingramont House, it was laid out in the mid nineteenth century, and once had three churches. Now only St. Mary's Episcopal Church survives on the right side (11). It was built through the influence of English officers at Hamilton Cavalry Barracks.

On the corner of Auchingramont Road and Union Street, is an interesting Dumfriesshire red sandstone, white harled, villa with a circular crow stepped door turret, called Linburn (No.51) designed by Gavin Paterson and erected in 1909 by Dr James Livingstone Loudon (12). Above the doorway is a "serpent", the symbol of medicine. His father, James Loudon M.D., built Linwood, the substantial red sandstone house, in 1872. Beyond these, at an angle to the street, is Cadzow Villa, much adapted and lying lower down. It is a much older property and, within its garden, there is a fine Cedar of Lebanon, known to have been planted by Bailie John Campbell in the 1770s.

Over on the left side of Union Street, the left corner at Auchingramont

Road is occupied by a large house originally called Netherlea, erected in 1860. It became offices for the Burgh of Hamilton, later Hamilton District Council. This is No.64.

James Salmon of Glasgow was the architect of Auchingramont Church with its tall steeple. It was used for public worship between 1860 and 1980 and was purchased by Hamilton District Council in 1982. It was later resold and converted into flats. The present Hamilton Manse, next door to the Church down Union Street, was erected in 1832, and for many years, was known as Burnside. It was purchased by the Parish Church in 1893 as a manse.

A plaque put up by Hamilton Civic Society relates that Cadzow Burn Bridge beyond here was widened in 1931. On the right hand side of the street, the side of Hamilton Grammar School can be seen (13). It was erected as Hamilton Academy in 1913, designed by Cullen, Lochhead and Brown and, like its lodge on the corner of Auchincampbell Road, the material used was Corncockle sandstone from Dumfriesshire. A better view can be had by crossing at the lights and walking on into Auchincampbell Road. The opposite corner here is known as Waugh's building and was formerly the Co-operative Bakery, erected in two phases in 1892 and 1921 to designs prepared by Gavin Paterson. Note the wheatsheaf on the corner turret. From here, as Union Street becomes Brandon Street, the corner building on the left at Hope Street can be seen, illustrating the effect of mining subsidence, not an uncommon feature in Hamilton at the beginning of the twentieth century (14).

Modern buildings and the Bus Station, on your right, replace the former railway goods yard. The car park area was the situation of the former Brandon Church.

Carry on to the Top Cross (15) and look at the remaining old buildings in Brandon Street, occupied by the Post Office, commercial premises and shops, consisting, in part, of the main Post Office, originally built for 'The Hamilton Herald'; the Post and Telegraph Office, opened in 1902, and the three storey Brandon Chambers (painted red), dating from 1898 and designed by Alexander Cullen.

Royal Buildings, the former Royal Hotel, which was erected by the Mackie family in 1874 to the design of Hamilton architect, William Moffat, stands on the corner to your right.

Slightly further down Duke Street is the Giffnock yellow sandstone fronted St John's Church, erected in 1834. The original St John's School, replaced by the Duke Street car park, stood beside it and was erected a year later. The rest of the street is of modern date.

Cross the road and proceed down Quarry Street. Quarry Street's left side has some very fine buildings but the Top Cross area in particular has some very distinguished architecture. The present Abbey National offices, which were erected in 1884 when James Robertson opened his Excelsior Stores, are distinctive. Brandon Tower (the grey sandstone buildings on the corner to the left), designed by Peat and Duncan and built in 1878, adds distinction to Hamilton's Top Cross. The Top Cross was created in 1830 when the Edinburgh/Ayr turnpike roads were linked by two new roads, Duke Street and Brandon Street (the Duke of Hamilton's English title), named in honour of the Duke who had supplied most of the money!

On the right is Baird's store, built on the site of the Old Town Hall with its fine steeple. The steeple went in 1951 and the rest of the building disappeared in 1964. Next to that is Sommerville Place with a cream sandstone building erected in 1878 at Nos. 91-99, and a fine pink sandstone building at Nos. 85-89. Nos. 41-49 Quarry Street is a three storey red sandstone building designed by Gavin Paterson in 1913 after a previous building had to be demolished because of fire damage. The building on the corner of Regents Way was also erected at that time and was designed by Alexander Cullen (16). On the other corner stands Victoria Buildings, built in yellow sandstone in 1887. On the left, the road is narrowed by the remnant of a "bottleneck" of surviving older houses (Nos. 2-26). Opposite this and round into Townhead Street is the building which 'Burton the Tailor' erected in 1925 and which was built from stone from the demolished Hamilton Palace. Quarry Street was widened at the same time. The street was named after Donaghadee Quarry, situated behind Kemp Street.

Turn left into Cadzow Street and then turn right down Campbell Street. At the corner with Postgate (where a sentry was posted to watch for strangers approaching the town) stands 'The Hamilton Advertiser' premises which incorporate the old Ebenezer Chapel, with which David Livingstone was associated.

Following round Postgate to the left on the corner with Church Street there stands the former Trades House dating back to 1816, used for Trades' and Societies' meetings and as a place of worship.

Turn right and downhill into Grammar School Square which takes its name from the school founded by the Duchess Anne in 1714, which stood there until 1930. The original Grammar School, founded in 1588, stood closer to the Palace by the Collegiate Church. Shielinghill takes its name from the town mill or sheeling, and Back o'Barns is where the grain was stored. This brings you back to the Museum.

THE GOOD OLD BURGH TOWN

The following is an extract from a song which was "sung with rapturous applause" at a dinner for the Town Council and Water Commissioners of Hamilton held on 7th November, 1867. It was sung to the tune of "The Good Old English Gentleman".

I'll sing you a song, my friends, of a good old Burgh town,
And of sixteen worthy gentlemen who yearly meet to drown
Their civic care, and toils that wear, and genially to crown
Their labours with a dinner good, and hear a song from BROWN.
The name of the town is HAMILTON, a good old Burgh town.

But tho' they are as valiant men as any in the nation,
And sit there at the head of all, they're not above their station:
As soon as fight, sure, any day, they'll offer arbitration,
(And in this, all besides, they have D. Parker's approbation).
These very prudent Councillors of that good old Burgh town.

Anon

THE HAMILTON ESTATE

Sharon Paton

"But Cadyow's towers, in ruins laid,
And vaults, by ivy mantled o'er,
Thrill to the music of the shade,
Or echo Evan's hoarser roar."

Sir Walter Scott

The M74 snakes through the heartland of Lanarkshire, cutting between the sprawling conurbations of Hamilton and Motherwell and carrying travellers and traders about their business. To many it is such an everyday sight most will hardly give a second thought to the landscape around them as it rushes past in a blur. Two distinctive landmarks, Chatelherault and Hamilton Mausoleum, may catch the eye and prompt a momentary thought as to the reason for their existence.

Origins of the Estate

Hamilton Estate was the primary domain of the Hamilton family in Lanarkshire. Surrounded by many other smaller estates, most of them in the possession of the Hamiltons or cadet branches of their extended family, changes in the development of Hamilton Estate helped to reshape the land and the lives of the people living in and around it.

As explained in the introductory chapter, the lands of Cadzow may once have served as royal hunting grounds, established by David I. There is strong evidence from Royal Charters issued by David I and Alexander II that a royal residence existed somewhere within the Barony of Cadzow, although any connection with the Cadzow Castle within Chatelherault Country Park remains doubtful. The faintly visible remnants of the Park Pale within the lands of the High Parks – a medieval earthen bank and ditch usually constructed to contain deer within a reserve – may be the only tangible clue to the estate's early origins.

After the Scottish victory at Bannockburn in 1314, Robert the Bruce gifted the Barony of Cadzow and a knighthood to Walter fitzGilbert de Hameldone, Castellon of Bothwell Castle. FitzGilbert de Hameldone's Anglo-Norman origins are somewhat obscure. The family are thought to have links with either the Earls of Leicester or the Umphravilles of

Northumberland, although they are not recorded in Scotland until 1294.

King James II invested Walter fitzGilbert's descendant, Sir James Hamilton of Cadzow, as 1st Lord Hamilton in 1445. Lord Hamilton's marriage to Princess Mary, sister of King James III, elevated the family to the pinnacle of social and political importance.

Gradually consolidating their influence on the area, the Hamiltons' estate encompassed several square miles of countryside surrounding the small town. From Bothwell Bridge, following the contour of the River Clyde to Dalserf in the Clyde Valley and the lands of Machan, the boundary enclosed the woodlands of the High Parks and lands of Thinacre, Quarter, Crookedstonemuir and Boghead. The lands continued around Barncluith and skirted around the little town of Hamilton before returning to Bothwell Bridge. The estate is divided by the natural course of the River Avon which cuts across it towards the River Clyde, so the low ground comprising the policies around Hamilton Palace was always referred to as the Low Parks and that of the higher ground overlooking the town as the High Parks.

Part of the privilege of status was the right granted by the Pope to Lord Hamilton in 1450-51 to build a new Collegiate Church next to his manorhouse. This substantial building replaced the old Parish Church of Cadyow (Cadzow).

The Collegiate Church was partially demolished after the completion of the town's new Parish Church by William Adam in 1734. The aisle containing the Hamilton family crypt remained until 1852 when the re-interment of the bodies in Hamilton Mausoleum allowed the removal of the last remnants of the old Church.

Castles and Palaces

The location of the Hamiltons' original dwelling within the Barony of Cadzow prior to the fourteenth century is unknown. In 1368, 'The Orchard' manor house is described as lying to the east of Cadzow (later Hamilton) town, but by the early sixteenth century, is located in the low-lying grounds near the town of Hamilton, which had evidently shifted south-west. It is from the time when Hamilton is established as a lordship in the fifteenth century that references relate to the family's principal dwelling as the 'Castle of Hamilton'. Later records give rise to some confusion. For example, by the sixteenth century, it is unclear as to whether reference is being made to a castle near the town or the castle in the High Parks. One appears to be a fortified stronghold, the other a more luxurious castle or palace replacing the original manor house near the town.

Records state that Hamilton (or Cadzow) Castle came under siege in 1515. Close proximity to the royal line and the power struggle which followed upon the death of James IV at Flodden, ensured that Hamilton lands were subject to attack and confiscation during the political instability in the sixteenth century. James Hamilton, 1st Earl of Arran, was deprived of the Sherriffdom of Lanark by his arch rival, the Duke of Albany, during King James V's minority. Arran wisely joined the King's successful coalition against Albany in 1525 and three years later gained the Douglas lands of Bothwell, after the King successfully defended himself against a charge of murdering a Douglas kinsman.

In the time of Scotland's governorship and regency under James Hamilton, 2nd Earl of Arran, the Earl used his influential position and wealth to construct a new 'Palice of Hamilton' between the mid 1540s and 1550s. Descriptions of the expensive embellishments – tapestries, glass, tame deer and seeds for the gardens – indicate a luxurious dwelling.

The Earl's eventual approval of the marriage of the young Mary Queen of Scots to the French Dauphin brought him the Duchy of Chatelherault in France. His opposition to Mary's marriage to Lord Darnley meant the forfeiture of Hamilton Castle in 1567, and his exile. This was short-lived and his later support of the Queen in Scotland initiated further political troubles affecting not only the family, but townspeople and tenants alike.

Mary spent her last night in Scotland at Hamilton, in 1568, on the eve of her army's defeat at the Battle of Langside. As a result of the Hamiltons' support for Mary, and in reprisal for the murder of the Regent Moray by a Hamilton kinsman, the Earl of Mar's troops raided the town, despoiling estate lands and burning the crops. In 1572, troops revisited the area in a repeat action where "Thair wes destroyit at this raid the haill fruittis about Hamiltoun and Boddelhaughe." The final siege of 1579 ended in victory to Regent Morton's troops and the total destruction of the castle by Act of Parliament.

When the family returned to greater favour in the reign of King James VI, John, 1st Marquis of Hamilton, rebuilt Hamilton Palace on its final site, around 1591, where it remained relatively unscathed through the troubled times in the seventeenth century.

The Covenanters played a major part in the political and civil upheavals of England and Scotland, and were a strong force in the West of Scotland. The Hamilton family, their estate tenants and the townspeople suffered the consequences, along with many others in the surrounding villages and towns.

Hamilton Palace, North Front 1919

45

The 1st Duke, as friend and confidant of Charles I, tried unsuccessfully to encourage moderation between opposing sides in Scotland, ending in his execution by Parliamentarians in 1649. The imposition of heavy fines and the occupation of the Palace by Cromwell's generals dealt a severe blow to the Hamiltons. During the occupation, the Duke's daughter and heiress, Duchess Anne, lived in the Woodhouse, a small house nestling within the secluded High Parks. After her marriage to William Douglas, Earl of Selkirk, Anne raised enough money to reclaim the Palace. On the restoration of Charles II in 1660, the family finally regained all of their property.

The Great Design

With the family's fortunes at their lowest ebb, the Duke and Duchess sold lands in order to repay all debts. They now possessed a shabby, old-fashioned home, intact, but exhibiting the neglect of enforced occupation. Its central courtyard with four corner turrets, the wooden balcony above the main entrance and the cluster of little thatched outhouses against the outer walls, now belonged to another era. Incorporating much of their own architectural knowledge, and under the direction of James Smith, the celebrated architect, the Palace was reborn as part of the Duke and Duchess's Great Design. This was their master plan to secure the future of the family, their estates and the town of Hamilton. From 1691 the south front and the west and east wings were rebuilt in stages, using most of the foundations and stone from the original building. The old north wing remained as part of the new design, but with a remodelled interior.

Building work progressed as speedily as possible, but always with an eye to the still troubled political scene. The Duke commented, "I do not intend to pull down a stone more until we are living in that now in hand and until we see a little more appearance of peaceable times." The new formal setting, along with the renowned kitchen and flower gardens, abundant orchards, and the pretty pond and statue garden, attracted the nobility from all over Scotland eager to learn from the Duke's passion for horticulture. His death in 1694 left the Duchess bereft but determined to continue with the plan.

The new Palace, on a size and scale previously unknown in the country, symbolised the re-established wealth and power of the Hamiltons, as well as reflecting their ambitions for the financial and industrial development of the town as a market centre. The older areas of Hamilton were gradually removed and resited in a continuing process of further improvements to the Palace and policies over the next 130 years.

In keeping with seventeenth century landscape fashion, great avenues and tree-lined walks formalised large areas of the policies. The origins of the picturesque 'Daurlin Ride' through the High Parks possibly dates from this period. A narrow coach ride through the woodland, it enabled observers, usually the ladies, to follow the progress of a hunt. Sections of the ride still exist as footpaths within Chatelherault Country Park. As a vast recreation ground the estate excelled, and the 3rd Duke had spent idyllic days in pursuit of hare coursing and hawking, his favourite sports.

Hamilton Palace served as a focus for the local economy and provided substantial employment for indoor and outdoor servants. Not simply a pleasure ground, the estate was self sufficient, providing the family with most of their requirements. Timber was sold for profit and estate tenants farmed their parcels of land, producing crops and raising sheep and cattle for sale in the local market. The Duchess received rents traditionally settled partially in cash and also in kind or 'kain', ranging from butter, eggs and grain to poultry, sheep and cattle. The estate provided game and the Palace had its own dairy and slaughterhouse. Local Hamilton merchants provided the luxury goods required to entertain the family and their numerous guests, although special items were brought from Edinburgh.

Cadzow Forest

This remnant of ancient oak woodland is the only example of its kind in Scotland. The small number of surviving Cadzow Oaks in the High Parks range from 800 years to the younger trees at 400 years old. With their bulbous, gnarled trunks they are an important habitat for hundreds of insects and other small invertebrates – the purple hairstreak butterfly, gall wasps, oak bark beetles and many species of spiders and moths.

The 1st Duke of Hamilton created large areas of woodland on the estate in the early seventeenth century. Described on a visit by Lord Fountainhall as having "great droves of hart and hind with young roes and fawns in companies of 100 and 60 together", the estate was renowned for its beauty.

Travel and the concept of tourism emerged in the eighteenth century when gentlemen and ladies of means, as well as poets, writers and artists, undertook lengthy journeys around Britain in search of the romantic or picturesque landscape. The unspoilt and isolated setting of Cadzow Forest and the High Parks fulfilled all the expectations of a procession of famous travellers to the area.

Cadzow Forest's beauty inspired the Cadzow Artists, a school of talented Scottish landscape painters formed in the mid-nineteenth century. The principal figures, Horatio McCulloch, Sam Bough, Alexander Fraser and Thomas Fairbairn, each exhibited highly acclaimed works depicting scenes in the High Parks, all of them staying in Hamilton at different periods, some for several years.

Hamilton Museum

David Crawford, a lawyer and the Hamiltons' Secretary, kept a watchful eye on the estate finances in the seventeenth and early eighteenth centuries. His fine classical town house, built in 1696, is situated in an area which was once the centre of town life on Muir Wynd, now Muir Street. David Crawford was a wealthy man and Hamilton Palace aside, his house was the finest private dwelling in the town. Purchased by the 8th Duke of Hamilton in 1784, 'Portland' became The Hamilton Arms Inn. The Assembly Room, with its elegant plaster work and the Fives Court, both to the rear of the main building, date from this period when the Inn became the focus of the town's social life.

The Inn was the main coaching house and mail stop in Hamilton en route from London to Glasgow. By 1835, the development of new roads in Hamilton meant the town centre had gradually moved away from the Inn which was now in a quiet backwater, and so it closed. The old stables made way for a new Riding School in 1837, part of the 10th Duke of Hamilton's aggrandisement of his palace and the surrounding policies. The Inn served as the Hamilton Estates Offices until Hamilton Burgh Council purchased the building for conversion into Hamilton Museum in 1964, and the Riding School became the home of the Cameronian (Scottish Rifles) Regimental Museum in 1983.

Enlightened Times

The development of Hamilton Palace and estate in the eighteenth century was very much a reflection of the social and economic developments taking place in Scotland. This was obvious in the changing architecture of the Palace and the growth of the economic strength of the town, but was more widely felt in the local community through the progress of agricultural practice and its impact in the community.

With the Palace externally complete by the beginning of the eighteenth century, Duchess Anne turned her attention to the estate. In 1708, landscape architect, Alexander Edward, drew up an ambitious formal setting for the magnificent new building. The plan included a great avenue

Chatelherault today

radiating north and south from the Palace, with elaborate formal parterres, tree-lined avenues, and sweeping vistas from the surrounding parklands giving views of the town and landscape. The death of the Duchess in 1716 meant that twenty more years would pass before her grandson James, 5th Duke of Hamilton, finalised the plan.

Chatelherault

The 5th Duke of Hamilton, who had spent most of his childhood in the loving care of his grandmother, was keen to fulfil her life's work and commissioned William Adam to produce suitable plans to complete the Palace and policies. Adam adapted Edward's original landscape design, terminating the unfinished South Great Avenue in 1732 with the elegant stretched facade of the Dogg Kennel – Chatelherault. A triumph of Georgian landscape architecture, Chatelherault was an effective eyecatcher as the onlooker gazed out along the distance of the tree-lined Grand Avenue.

An unusual and distinctive building with its four pavilions and scalloped screen wall, Chatelherault's elevated position gives sweeping views of the surrounding countryside. This view once encompassed the formal garden of the Palace dotted with elegant little temples and an ornamental canal and

49

cascade, fed by the diverted Cadzow Burn and flowing into the River Clyde. Behind Chatelherault stretches the expanse of natural woodland along the Avon Gorge. Adam's landscape of contrasts introduced innovative elements of freedom and romanticism, a reflection of ideals embraced enthusiastically in the eighteenth century. This contrast also carries into the building itself, both in the dual function of summer palace and hunting lodge with its elaborately decorated apartments, and as a very utilitarian dog kennel, originally housing the 5th Duke's pack of hunting dogs.

Adam also refurbished several of the principal apartments in Hamilton Palace, replacing the heavier seventeenth century decor with a lighter, more stylish form. The 5th Duke's death in 1743 halted Adam's plans for the new North and South fronts of Hamilton Palace. His elegant exterior design would have been the final visual triumph of such a grandiose landscape plan.

Agriculture

At the beginning of the eighteenth century, agricultural practice on the Hamilton estate, as in the rest of Scotland, was still relatively primitive. Tenants farmed with heavy wooden ploughs creating raised ridge and furrow patterns for hand-sown crops. Remnants of these early rig and furrows still exist in small fields around the High Parks. The flat plains of the Low Parks near the River Clyde provided the tenants leasing the individual fields with rich grazing areas, and outlying sections of the estate were let as small farms. General Roy's map of 1747 indicates the early beginnings of the enclosure system on the estate starting with the lands around the Palace.

John Burrel, the Duke's 'overseer of all outworks' and a man of immense talents, surveyed the estate in 1763 with a view to introducing major new land improvements. This would lead the way to more commercial farming practice and increased profitability for the estate. Tenants followed a strict system of rules. If they carried out the improvements themselves, they qualified for an 'improved rent' – a reduction. Burrel insisted on grain crops for the first few years in the High and Low Parks to improve soil. He regarded tree nurseries as essential, providing the hawthorn hedging to enclose the fields, and field drains were a necessity. The Duke's limeworks at Boghead near Quarter supplied the lime fertiliser to improve soil condition, a revolutionary new practice which vastly increased crop yields.

Victorian Heyday

The last remnants of old Hamilton were finally removed in the 1820s on the eve of the final and grandest transformation of Hamilton Palace. Alexander, 10th Duke of Hamilton, was influenced by his family's royal ancestry and inspired by the marvellous architecture and art collections of European royalty which he viewed on his social tours. A cultured and knowledgeable collector himself, he endeavoured to build a Palace of unequalled grandeur and housing an unrivalled collection of art and antiquities. David Hamilton, the architect, revised William Adam's plans for the Palace, and work progressed for the next twenty years, producing a suitable showpiece for the Duke.

The Low Parks underwent a transformation from formal Georgian splendour to a great Victorian park, complete with grand fountain, statues and the fussily planted flower beds so typical of that era. The enormity of the Palace, the richness of the interiors, the sumptuous lifestyle within and the processions of Royal visitors soon earned the Duke the nickname of 'Il Magnifico'. Hamilton Mausoleum, built for the Duke between 1845 and 1856 as a final resting place and monument to the Hamilton family, is one of the most costly private tombs ever built in the country. Today it dominates the landscape surrounding the M74. As a magnificent example of a wealthy man's memorial and an illustration of the nineteenth century attitude to death, it serves as a lasting reminder of Alexander's aspirations.

A grand procession of British and European royal heads of state visited Hamilton Palace. The 11th Duke's wife, Princess Marie of Baden and cousin of Napoleon III of France, linked the family to most of the crowned heads of Europe. The High Parks remained a preserve of the family principally for picnics rather than hunting – a favourite spot next to Cadzow Castle was known as the Castle Green – but on important social occasions and Royal visits, the customary shooting party spent a day or two in pursuit of game.

Two interesting tributes to William, 11th Duke of Hamilton, stand near Chatelherault. In 1863, the Duke's Bridge formed a permanent crossing point over the River Avon near Cadzow Castle. Replacing the traditional ford located a few yards further upstream, it commemorates the 11th Duke's death in the same year. The Duke's Monument at Barncluith, a classical rotunda of granite and stone, was built by public subscription in 1869 and perches on the edge of a steep section of the Avon Gorge.

A Sad Ending

The enormous expense incurred by the 10th Duke in building the Palace, and the debts incurred by his successors, left the estate finances in a precarious position. A huge sale of art held at the Palace in 1882 signified the beginning of the end for the Hamilton Estate.

Coal mining, commencing in the Low Parks in 1882, reached the unworked coal around the Palace in 1916. The Hamilton family's decision to leave the Palace and move to Dungavel Lodge near Strathaven opened the way to full-scale mining shortly after, despite a last ditch attempt to halt the works. A final sale of treasures in 1919 was followed by ten years of gradual demolition beginning in 1922. Thus all traces of Hamilton Palace were wiped away, as the coal industry slowly reduced the Low Parks to a shadow of its former glory.

The High Parks remained in the ownership of the Hamilton family, although Chatelherault was no longer home to estate workers. A fire damaged most of the decorative apartments in the west wing in the mid 1960s, and then the death of the old watchman left the building unguarded. Sand quarrying of the land immediately surrounding Chatelherault now threatened its very existence. The Hamiltons finally moved to Lennoxlove House, near Haddington, in 1972. Following the death of the 14th Duke, the High Parks was auctioned in lots to resolve the problem of death duties. Chatelherault, now reduced to ruins, was purchased by the Scottish Office in 1978, along with the Avon Gorge, with a view to restoration. After an eight year programme of work, the building and parkland opened to the public in 1987.

Today, Chatelherault and the Country Park are managed by Hamilton District Council.

AN EXCURSION TO
THE HIGH PARKS

The following poem appeared in "The Hamilton Advertiser" in July, 1856.

When we had got our teas and coffees
We went down to the Duke's office
And got our order for the Parks
On which we will make some remarks.
We started at the chap o' ten
With four ladies and two men
One girl, three lassies and a youth
And went up to Barncluith
And in the garden there did grow
A lot of odd bushes in a row
And down below us was the Avon
That makes the ginger-bread at Strathaven
And also too we saw the railway
Which goes on to the pits the whole way.
We also did perceive a mill
That goes when it is not standing still.
We saw two bridges and a toll
And that I think is most the whole.
And then went to a wooden gate
To see the oaks so big and great
And when we went about a mile
We seen t'em all in splendid style.
Some were broad and some were long
And some we thought did not look strong.
You do not need for to be told
That all of them were very old.
But one thing I must not pass by
And that of course is the wild kye
With noses and skins so white
They were an extraordinary sight.

Then unto Cadzow we did go
Which is a ruin you must know
And though so old, to me it was new
And presented an extensive view.
The Avon it was down below
And opposite was Shatelyrow.
Far off we could behold the deer
As they did not come very near
And as the day was wearing on
We came back to Hamilton
Much pleased with everything we saw that day
And the Duke's kindness every way.

Anon

BLANTYRE

Neil Gordon

I make no pretensions that this is a complete history of Blantyre. The object is to give in a limited space some idea of the main events in our town's history that brought our locality to what it is today.

Blantyre Pre 1785

Blantyre is a long narrow strip of land eight miles south of Glasgow, between East Kilbride and Hamilton. It measures six and a quarter miles north to south and two and a half miles at its widest point, east to west. Its main boundaries are the River Calder to the west and the River Clyde to the north and east.

Evidence of man's inhabitation of Blantyre can be traced to the Bronze Age fort of Camp Knowe at Calderside, Auchentibber. Many Bronze Age graves have been found throughout the area. All of Britain, from the Bronze Age to the Roman Occupation, was inhabited by Welsh speaking ancient Briton tribes. Blantyre was part of the Kingdom of Cumbria inhabited by the Damnonii tribe whose northern capital was Alcluyd (two Welsh words meaning Rock of Clyde). Their kingdom's southern border was on the River Ribble in Lancashire, England. The present day name for Alcluyd is Dumbarton and was taken from the Gaelic speaking Scots who referred to Alcluyd as Dun-Britton (Fort of the Britons). There have been various suggestions as to the definition of the name Blantyre. From the evidence I have mentioned, I believe it is reasonable to assume that Blantyre was an ancient British settlement and was built around the Old Blantyre Kirk Yard which may have been a druid religious circle. The Kirk Yard is a large man-made eight foot high mound of earth and, if it was a druid circle, it would have been the centre of the settlement's religious activities. The old sixteenth century communion cups belonging to the Old Parish Church have no letter E in the spelling of BLANTYRE. I would suggest that the old spelling Blantyr is a gaelic corruption of LLANTYR. Llantyr contains two Welsh words – LLAN meaning consecrated and TYR meaning ground/land, the consecrated/church ground being the Old Kirk Yard at High Blantyre Cross. Through time the Britons were dispersed from the area and those that remained were converted to Christianity and continued to use their original pagan consecrated ground by constructing a church there. At least two churches have stood in the Old Kirk Yard. The barbaric tongue (Welsh) was still in use in some remote areas of Scotland at the time of the Reformation in the sixteenth century. There are several other theories as to the origin of the name Blantyre. The Reverend Stevenson, writing in 1790, suggested that it was two Gaelic words meaning Warm Retreat. Another suggestion, from the Reverend Wright, writing in 1895, was that it was Gaelic, meaning Field of The Holy Men.

The earliest written record of the name Blantyre was in 1275 where the Priory was included in a list of Scottish ecclesiastical establishments which were taxed by Pope Clement IV to raise money to finance yet another crusade against the Saracens. This document was known as Bagimond's Roll, named after the Pope's emissary, Baiamund De Vicci, who was sent to collect the hated tax. The Priory was almost certainly mentioned in a previous list issued by Pope Innocent IV in 1254 to finance an earlier crusade. Most of the early priors are recorded as having attended Scottish parliaments and being involved in many important incidents in Scottish history. Blantyre Priory stood on Blantyr Craig, the high cliff directly opposite Bothwell Castle, and was founded between 1238 and 1249. The Priory was a cell of the Augustinian Canon of Jedburgh Abbey who also used it over the years as a retreat from the wars between England and Scotland. The last Roman Catholic Prior was William Chirnside who conformed to the new religion and became the first Protestant minister in Blantyre in 1567. It was he who purchased the old communion cups for the converted Catholic Church that stood in the Old Kirk Yard at Blantyre Village, two miles south of the Priory at High Blantyre Cross.

In 1595, after the suppression of the Roman Catholic Church by James VI, the Priory and its lands were bestowed by the King on his cousin, Walter Stuart, the Treasurer of Scotland who was created a Peer of the Realm and took the title Lord Blantyr on 10th July, 1606. It is thought that the first five Lords of Blantyre resided at Blantyre Priory. The fifth Lord Blantyre built a new family home in Renfrew. This house is now the Erskine Hospital for disabled soldiers. The money for the new home was left to the fifth Lord Blantyre by the Duchess of Richmond, the grand-daughter of the first Lord Blantyre, and it is thought that she was born at Blantyre Priory. The Duchess was a member of the royal court of King Charles II and became one of his many mistresses, the most famous being Nell Gwynne. Frances, by all accounts, was one of the beauties of her day and was known throughout the royal courts of Europe as La Belle Stuart. A full length painting of Frances can be seen at Hampton Court, London. When King Charles instructed the Royal Mint to produce a new penny and halfpenny coin, the emblem chosen for the new coins was the figure of Brittania. It was his favourite, Frances Stuart, that Charles asked to model as Brittania and she can still be seen on our present day coinage.

In 1314, Robert the Bruce defeated the English army at the Battle of Bannockburn. One of his generals was his nephew, Thomas Randolph, the Earl of Moray. The Barony of Blantyre was gifted by the King to Randolph for services rendered at this famous battle. After the death of Bruce, Thomas Randolph was appointed Regent of Scotland during the minority of Bruce's son, King David II, and he proved to be a wise and just ruler. The Barony consisted of small hamlets, namely Barnhill, Hunthill, Auchinraith, Auchentibber, Blantyre Priory and Kirkton, the old town centre at High Blantyre Cross. The population of Blantyre before 1780 was around five hundred. The inhabitants, as in other towns and villages, had to observe Royal Proclamations, such as one that instructed that the 'Lower Classes' should practise archery during holidays and Sundays after divine service. Archery practice took place in a large field opposite the Old Parish Church, known as Archer's Croft. Archer's Croft was divided into two areas when a railway was constructed across the field to take the line over the River Calder to East Kilbride. The columns of the old viaduct bridge can still be seen adjacent to Hunthill football fields and from Stoneymeadow Road.

Calder Mills

There were six mills on the River Calder, namely the Mavis Mill, Bardyke (also known as the Black Mill), Dyesholm Mill, Millheugh, Crossbasket and one unnamed mill south of the General's Bridge. All grain produced by the farmers had to be taken to the local mills as part of their tenancy agreement with the land owner. The Lords of Blantyre received a percentage of the grain as rent from the farmers and millers. It guaranteed work to the millers and ensured that the farmers had a mill close at hand to grind their grain. The landowner, the millers and farmers were in a way dependent on each other. The mills that worked under the above conditions were known as Astricted Mills.

School Children at Barnhill, Blantyre 1880

High Blantyre Cross c1900

59

Blantyre Mills

The arrival in 1785 of David Dale and the construction of his first cotton spinning mill changed the environment literally overnight. The quiet, peaceful, rural community disappeared as the industrial revolution took its grip on the town. A second spinning mill was constructed in 1791 causing another surge in the population. Half the population at this time were employed at the Blantyre Mills. Dale's original partner, John Kay, the inventor of the flying shuttle, dropped out of the partnership and was replaced by Henry Monteith who expanded the works for the third time. Dale, in his turn, sold out to Monteith in 1792 and it was to remain in the Monteith family until 1873. Many improvements were carried out, including the construction of a self contained village with toll gates situated at the junction of Station Road with Rosebank Avenue and Knightswood Terrace. These gates were closed at 10.00 pm each evening. By 1794 the roads had improved and the Works village had become larger than the main town centre at Kirkton, High Blantyre. Business boomed at the Works so much that, in 1813, a weaving factory containing 463 looms, driven partly by water and partly by steam engine, was opened. A school and chapel were built in 1828. The village had a company-owned shop, and it was a complete new town owned by the company.

The working day at the mills was long and hard. The work force, which contained children as young as six years old, were awakened at 5.30 am by the ringing of the works bell. Work commenced at 6.00 am with a breakfast break at 8.00 am and a lunch break at mid-day lasting for one hour. There was one other meal break in the late afternoon. The working day finished at 8.00 pm. The working hours were reduced by an Act of Parliament in 1834. The mill owners found it difficult to recruit labour for its ever-expanding works. They would travel to Greenock and Leith docks and offer employment and homes to the unfortunate crofters who had been evicted from their houses by their landlords during the infamous Highland Clearances and were en route to America. Many accepted and were grateful for the opportunity to stay in the land of their birth.

The mill owner also had children in his labour force known as Barrack Children. These were orphans between the ages of six and twelve who had been adopted from the parish authorities by the Manager of Blantyre Works. The mill owner had to undertake to clothe them, provide them with a good education, living quarters and attend to their health and spiritual needs. Although we may consider the long working day and their environment as harsh, the workers and the Barrack Children considered themselves fortunate to live and work at Blantyre Mills. The long working day meant that there was very little time for personal pursuits. Saturday was considered a relatively short working day as they only worked nine hours. Sunday, of course, being the Sabbath and keenly observed, meant that the Barrack Children had little time to play the usual children's games. The first school at the Work's Village was in two rooms on the ground floor of Shuttle Row. The children attended this school after work between 8.00 pm and 10.00 pm.

Many workers lived to a great age and in one case a mill mechanic was still working at the age of ninety four. The only other industry in the parish at this time other than the cotton mills and farming was the mining of large deposits of limestone and ironstone at Auchentibber. The demise of the mills was caused through the decline in the cotton industry. Production ceased at Blantyre Mills in 1903 and the company was liquidated in 1904.

David Livingstone

Blantyre's most famous son, David Livingstone, was born in a single end on the third floor of Shuttle Row on 19th March, 1813. There is no need to comment here on his famous exploits in Africa as these are well documented and known to people throughout the world. Blantyre will forever be associated with the name David Livingstone. There is one little known local event concerning Livingstone that might be worth noting. It is generally thought that Livingstone did not visit Blantyre on his return from Africa but that is not the case as the following events will prove. Livingstone only returned home from Africa on two occasions. On his first trip he travelled to Hamilton to visit his mother who had moved to a cottage at Peacock Cross in 1839 prior to his leaving for Africa. Major Ness, the headmaster of Blantyre Works School, on learning of the pending visit, wrote to Livingstone requesting him to visit Blantyre and give an address to the Blantye Literary & Scientific Institute. Livingstone politely refused this invitation.

Major Ness was determined that the great man would visit his birthplace and asked Livingstone's mother to use her influence with her son to come to Blantyre. When Livingstone arrived at his mother's home in Hamilton she immediately sent word to Ness that David had arrived the previous night and that he should again write to Livingstone requesting a visit to Blantyre. Major Ness took her advice and sent the letter with Archie Campbell, an old boyhood friend of Livingstone. The ploy succeeded and the great man agreed to come to the meeting.

The date set for the soiree was 31st December, 1856, at Blantyre Works School/Chapel. Doors to open at 5.30 pm. Tea to be served at 6.00 pm precisely. At this time Blantyre, according to Ness, was the residence of many commercial gentlemen who had businesses in Glasgow and the audience present at the soiree represented not only the inhabitants of Blantyre but many distinguished people from other areas. Major Ness recalled that, during his speech, Livingstone had been relating some of his experiences in Africa, when he suddenly stopped and appeared confused. A painful silence fell over the audience. Someone in the hall, by way of encouragement, shouted, "Spit it out, Dr Livingstone." Livingstone said "Excuse me, ladies and gentlemen, but you do not know the mental agony I am suffering. I am speaking to you in English, but at the same time I am thinking my subject in African, and I am translating my words into English. I have been sixteen years in Africa and during that time I have scarcely looked upon the face of a white man. Do you wonder that I have almost forgotten my mother tongue?" Encouraged, Livingstone went on to finish his speech.

David Livingstone can justifiably be considered as one of the greatest explorers/pioneers in history. His adventures caught the imagination of people throughout the world. Livingstone's journeys into the vast unknown African interior can be compared with any expedition ever undertaken, even Neil Armstrong's journey to the moon. Armstrong's every movement was monitored and controlled by a vast back-up team. Livingstone, on the other hand, went alone into Africa's unchartered regions with no back-up. Armstrong's journey took but a few days, Livingstone's journeys took a lifetime.

Coal Industry

Local mining existed in Hamilton and Cambuslang from 1860. It was not until 1873 that test borings discovered seven seams of coal in the Blantyre area. Five companies sunk pits in Blantyre, the three largest being Murray and Cunningham, William Dixon and William Baird. Between them these companies established eight collieries. The coming of the mining industry began a great social change in the town and it came at a time when output at Blantyre Mills was declining. The mines, by polluting the River Clyde, had hastened their closure by the turn of the twentieth century. The mill workers then turned to the coal industry for employment. There was a great demand for labour in the new industry. The inflow of workers pushed the population up dramatically. In 1851, before the discovery of coal, the population numbered 2,848. By 1881, ten years after the first pits were sunk, the population had increased to a total of 9,760. In 1904, just thirty three years after coal production had commenced, the population had risen from 2,848 inhabitants to 15,000. The mine owners constructed rows of cottages, mainly in the Stonefield area. These were built on both sides of Glasgow Road. Bairds Rows were constructed in the area between the East Kilbride Expressway and Forrest Street. There were three rows of houses that ran parallel to Glasgow Road and the railway line. Murray and Cunningham built a row of houses on Auchinraith Road at the top of Craig Street, close by Auchinraith Colliery. The main housing was Murray's Rows which occupied both sides of the present day Elm Street. From 1870, Main Street, High Blantyre and Glasgow Road in Stonefield were developed to provide shops to service the population and thus the town expanded. By the mid 1950s, all of Blantyre's collieries had closed and most of the miners had either left the Blantyre area to find work in the Fife coalfields or were bussed to mines in adjacent districts.

There was one unfortunate incident in those early days of the mines. In May, 1878, the miners at Dixon's Collieries came out on strike for an increase in wages. The mine owners refused, and threatened to dismiss the men and evict them from their homes. Due to this threat some miners returned to work only to find that their wages had been cut as a punishment for striking and there was nothing they could do about it. When the mines had opened a few years earlier, there had been a great influx of poor Irish peasants to the Lanarkshire mine fields, and it was to Ireland the owners turned again for replacement labour after they had evicted the remaining strikers. At the time of the strike there was a potato famine in Ireland and this was causing great suffering and starvation amongst the peasants there. Naturally these men jumped at the chance of a job and a home in Blantyre. They were paid the cut rate of pay that the returning strikers had been forced to accept. Compared to their present plight this offer was a heaven-sent opportunity to these Irish families. The evicted miners, of course, resented the immigrants who had broken the strike and caused them to lose their jobs and homes. The Irish families brought with them their own customs and their Roman Catholic religion to a predominantly Presbyterian community. Owing to all these facts there was a great deal of resentment and antagonism in Blantyre for many years following this incident. Looking back, you can understand the feelings of the families on both sides of the dispute. On the one hand the Irishmen had saved their families from possible death by starvation. Who could condemn them for that? On the other hand the Blantyre miners lost their jobs and homes and were turned destitute into the street. Who could blame them for feeling bitter about the Irish immigrants? The only winners were the mine owners who had played one side against the other.

Blantyre Disaster

All the collieries in the Lanarkshire coal belt were notorious for firedamp. This gas on many occasions ignited in various pits causing injury and death to many miners but these incidents were small when compared to the "Blantyre Calamity". It is claimed that mining regulations were sometimes ignored by the mine owners, in the rush to extract the coal as quickly as possible, at the cheapest price, in order to beat their competitors. At 8.45 am on Monday, 22nd October, 1877, Dixon's Pit exploded, caused by the lack of ventilation in the mine. A ventilation furnace had been allowed to burn down and had not been stoked up for the commencement of the day-shift. This allowed a lethal build-up of firedamp which exploded. Of the 233 men and boys who descended the pit at 5.30 am that morning, only twenty four survived. The court of enquiry that followed the disaster suggested that a spark or naked light from a candle on a miner's hat had ignited the firedamp. It was to be some years later before it was discovered that it was not the firedamp alone that caused the explosions in those early pits. It was found that coal dust was as explosive as dynamite in certain circumstances. The events and conditions at Dixon's Pit that morning caused the biggest colliery disaster in Scottish history and the second largest in Britain. Major Ness who, by this time, was the headmaster of the new Stonefield Public School, recalled that he first heard of the disaster when a distraught woman rushed into his room crying "Maister, Maister, let the weans oot, their faithers are a' deid. Dixon's has blasted". A disaster fund was set up and money was received from all over the country. It is interesting to note that Queen Victoria donated mourning dresses for the widows. It was thought that a donation of money would have been more appropriate. The site of Dixon's Colliery explosion is on the Hillhouse Road, midway between the roundabouts at the Industrial Estate and Douglas Street.

The Ejection of the Blantyre Widows

Six months after the explosion, thirty four widows, whose husbands had been killed in the disaster, appeared at Hamilton Sheriff Court. They had previously received letters from the colliery owners informing them that they must leave their tied cottages. Having failed to do so, William Dixon Limited had raised summonses against them.

When asked by the Sheriff why they had not vacated their homes, each widow stated that they did not have the means with which to pay a rent. The Sheriff asked, "Are you not getting enough money from the relief fund?" Each widow replied "I have not have the means to pay a rent with."

The Sheriff stated that it was out of kindness that the company had allowed them to remain in their houses for so long. One widow claimed that they had a cruel way of showing their kindness and that the firm should have carried out the evictions on the day of the explosion as the public would have taken her by the hand.

The Sheriff stated that he could scarcely agree with her and suggested that both the firm and the public had been extremely kind and generous. He then decreed that the thirty four widows and their children should be removed from their homes in two weeks time, on 28th May, 1878.

The evictions were carried out and replacement miners were allocated their homes. No-one knows what became of these unfortunate widows and their children. In all probability they had to seek accommodation in the Poor House. The ejection of the Blantyre widows was a sad and disgraceful end to the tragic story of the Blantyre explosion.

I was honoured when I was asked to design the monument that was unveiled on 22nd October, 1977, at High Blantyre Cross to commemorate the centenary of the Blantyre Explosion. I feel that the monument today has an added responsibility as it is the only visible structure within the community that will remind future generations of Blantyre's coal mining heritage. Blantyre's pit bings that stood for decades like pyramids dominating the town's landscape have now disappeared.

Blantyre Today

Redevelopment of the town centre saw the demolition of the old tenement buildings at Glasgow Road to make way for the new centralised Clydeview shopping centre, opened in October, 1980, and followed by the construction of Blantyre Sports Centre which opened in June, 1982. Since the demise of the coal industry, Blantyre has almost turned full circle, while not exactly to the quiet peaceful rural village of yesteryear but to a pleasant, open-plan community. The economy of the town is now largely based upon factory units at High Blantyre Industrial Estate where a variety of companies are engaged in businesses such as light engineering, printing and computer services etc, and are now firmly established within the community. Adjacent to the industrial estate and at present under construction is the new Hamilton International Business Park which, along with an excellent local road network linking with the national motorway system, should ensure that business companies will continue to locate within our community.

Today is tomorrow's history and I am confident that some future Blantyre historian will look favourably on our efforts to advance our town with confidence to a prosperous future in the new millennium.

BLACK AGNES

Agnes, Countess of Dunbar (d. 1369), was the daughter of Thomas Randolph, Earl of Moray and the wife of Patrick, Earl of March and Dunbar. Known as Black Agnes because of her dark hair and complexion and Lady of Blantyre from the family's connections with the Barony of Blantyre, Agnes became famous for her defence, in her husband's absence, of Dunbar Castle against the English, in 1338. As each enemy cannon ball scored a hit, she and her maids would dust the broken masonry off the battlements with their handkerchiefs! The following is part of a ballad written at the time in praise of Black Agnes.

She kept a stir in tower and trench,
The brawling, boisterous Scottish wench;
Came I early, came I late,
I found Agnes at the gate.

Anon

David Livingstone

DAVID LIVINGSTONE

The Scottish National Memorial to David Livingstone Trust

The Blantyre Cotton Spinning Mill - Birthplace of David Livingstone

The birthplace of the famous medical missionary and explorer, Dr David Livingstone, in the tall tenement at the end of Shuttle Row in Blantyre, is now part of a museum and visitor attraction centre, celebrating the life and works of this extraordinary man.

The building was erected, in the Scottish baronial style, about 1785 and is the last remaining of the "Rows" built to house employees of the Blantyre Cotton Spinning Works. Founded by David Dale and sold to James Monteith of Anderson, the Blantyre cotton mill was one of the first of the pioneering experiments in Scotland providing housing and education for the workers.

Shuttle Row consisted of twenty four single room houses, each room only fourteen feet by ten feet with an open fireplace for cooking. Entire families lived, ate and slept in these cramped and overcrowded conditions. Some families even kept poultry and animals in their tiny one-bedroomed houses. Each house had two bed recesses and a separate moveable "Hurley" bed which was pulled out into the middle of the room at night. There was no piped water in the building, and slops and rubbish were disposed of into "jawboxes" - sluice holes cut into the sides of communal circular staircases - to be drained into cess pits at the rear of the building.

Such conditions might shock today, but the Blantyre Mills provided a higher standard of workers' accommodation than would have been found in many other industrialised areas. The image of "dark satanic mills" as has been described in the cotton industry elsewhere, was not apparent in Blantyre, but the strict company regulations, hazardous working conditions and long hours nevertheless seem, by modern standards, quite appalling.

75% of the work force of the Blantyre Cotton Mill were children, who were employed as "piecers", their job being to "piece" together broken threads on the spinning machines, essential to avoid flaws on the finished yarn. Injuries from the moving machinery and beatings by adult spinners eager to improve their output were commonplace, while the deafening noise of the water-driven machinery and the practice of steam heating the workspace to 80-90°F to improve the thread quality made working conditions far from pleasant.

All employees, both adults and children, worked a six day week, from 6.00 am till 8.00 pm, with half an hour for breakfast and an hour for lunch. Children were given the opportunity of attending the company school after work from 8.00 pm till 10.00 pm. Recession due to the Napoleonic Wars and cotton shortages were claimed by the management to prevent any reduction in working hours. Such problems did not, however, prevent the mill owner, Henry Monteith, from earning a personal fortune of £80,000 in five supposedly difficult years.

The Blantyre Cotton Works continued to expand under the Monteith family, with the construction of further factory extensions, a chapel/school room and library in 1828 and the Blantyre Works village in 1830 to accommodate more workers needed for increased production.

David Livingstone - from Mill Boy to Missionary

It was into this grim environment that David Livingstone was born on 19th March, 1813, in one of the single apartments on the second floor of the tenement block in Shuttle Row, the second in a family of five children.

By the age of ten he was working as a piecer in the mill but was already showing the traits which would set him aside from other men, an inner drive and a self reliant single mindedness that could easily be called stubborn. His early interests in science and natural history, and reading tales of Captain Cook's travels, were frowned on by his strictly religious father who was suspicious of the new scientific philosophies. Livingstone later recalled that the last beating he received from his father was for refusing to read Wilberforce's "Practical Christianity". Such disagreements were, however, later to be resolved.

Throughout Livingstone's remarkable and complex career, he never forgot his humble origins and arduous childhood in Blantyre's Cotton Mill, and he often reminisced and compared scenery in Africa to the countryside of the Clyde Valley where he wandered as a boy. His interest in natural history was to stay with him throughout his life and in Africa he was to discover plants and animals previously unknown to science.

Livingstone made the most of the schooling that was offered to him, though his spelling remained erratic and his grammar far from perfect, even later in life. From an early age he saw education as a way of avoiding a life of drudgery amongst the clanking machinery in the Blantyre mills. He regularly propped up a book near the spinning machines so that he could study subjects such as Latin while he worked, and he was not dissuaded from his ambitions by the scoffing of his peers. At nineteen years old, he was promoted to the better paid post of spinner but he was still working in the mills at the age of twenty one with little opportunity for the freedom that he sought.

At this point he happened to read a pamphlet by Karl Gutzlaff which his father had brought back from church. It was an appeal for "medical missionaries" to be sent to China. Livingstone immediately realised that here was a way in which science and religion might be combined in a career that would have his father's approval. However, even after convincing his father and gaining financial assistance from his brother, it was to be a further two years before Livingstone had sufficient funds to embark on a medical training, and even then he had to continue working in the mills whenever he could to support his studies.

In the autumn of 1836, David Livingstone and his father Neal trudged through early heavy snowfalls to Glasgow, eventually finding meagre lodgings for David in Rotten Row. David Livingstone would make this eight mile journey on foot from Blantyre every Monday morning during the winter to study at Anderson College, a Medical School near George Square. During this period, he met James Young of Kelly, a chemist who invented the process for distilling oil from shale. Livingstone nicknamed him "Sir Paraffin". James Young remained a life-long friend and correspondent and would later finance Livingstone's last expedition.

While he was undergoing his medical training, Livingstone also studied Greek at Glasgow University and attended lectures in theology. He applied to, and was accepted by, the London Missionary Society and was sent for training to Chipping Ongar in Essex. Later, he continued his medical studies in London and finally returned to Scotland to sit his examinations at the Faculty of Physicians and Surgeons in Glasgow in 1840.

While Livingstone had always had a great interest in scientific matters, his theological training with the London Missionary Society did not go at all smoothly and there were some considerable reservations as to his suitability as a missionary even after additional tuition. His lack of a formal education, his accent, gruff manner and lack of experience in public speaking gave him a substantial handicap compared with other students. Indeed, on one occasion, members of a congregation told him that if they "knew he was to preach again they would not enter the chapel." Despite all the problems he was eventually considered to be ready and on 20 November, 1840, was officially ordained at Albion Chapel, Finsbury in London.

While in London he met a fellow Scot, Dr Robert Moffat, a well known and respected missionary who was home on leave from the mission station at Kuruman, some 500 miles north of Cape Town. Moffat's accounts of southern Africa fired Livingstone's imagination and he asked Moffat if he thought he "would do for Africa". "Yes," Moffat replied "if you are prepared to leave occupied land and push to the North". The London Missionary Society agreed to Livingstone's request and on 8th December, 1840, aged 27, he sailed from London aboard "The George".

Livingstone in Africa

The Africa on the eve of Livingstone's arrival, as viewed through Victorian eyes, was a vast alien world - the Dark Continent. This is somewhat surprising when it is realised that Portuguese, Dutch and British settlements had existed at various points around the coasts for over 200 years. But almost nothing was known of central Africa and the maps of the period contained only hypothetical drawings of deserts and mountains added at the artist's discretion. The only exception was the southern tip of the continent where the climate and the absence of malaria and tsetse fly had encouraged some expansion. When Dr David Livingstone landed at Simon's Bay on 15 March, 1841, there was little indication that he was to become a major player in the shaping of the future of the African continent.

It is a common misconception that Livingstone was the first person to bring Christianity to Africa. In fact, George Schmidt had baptised slaves at the Cape a century before Livingstone arrived and the London Missionary Society already had twenty missionaries in South Africa when Livingstone was tying his first thread in the mills at Blantyre. Livingstone was posted to Robert Moffat's mission station, some 500 miles from the coast. The settled life of neatly tended orchards and gardens at Kuruman was hardly what Livingstone had expected and he was shocked to find that after twenty years work Moffat had less than forty converts. It was not long before he started to look to make some impact further afield.

In fact, Livingstone's career in Africa almost came to an untimely end when he was attacked and badly mauled by a lion. After he recovered he married Moffat's daughter, Mary. He was soon to become aware of the practical difficulties of interesting Africans in Christianity, particularly in tribal cultures where polygamy was the norm. Even when villages were apparently enthusiastic about having a resident missionary, it often had more to do with protection from Boer settlers or other tribes than any interest in the Christian message. After seven years in Africa Livingstone had only made one convert and had come to realise that as a resident missionary he was unlikely to make any significant impact on Africa.

Early on he had acquired a taste for exploring and he began to see a role for himself in opening up a route to the interior for others to follow so that "Christianity and Commerce" would flourish and thereby eradicate slavery which was endemic in Africa. After a near disaster when his family almost died of thirst in the Kalihari desert, Livingstone sent his wife and children to Scotland and embarked on the epic trans-continental journey which was to make him world famous. Mary Livingstone and their four children arrived in Hamilton to stay with Livingstone's parents and his two spinster sisters at Ulva Cottage near Peacock Cross. Unfortunately, the arrangement was not successful as Mary Livingstone did not get on well with her in-laws and her eldest son Robert became very unruly. Within six months she had left the area and moved south with the children to Hackney near London to what was to become for her a life of loneliness, depression and secret alcoholism.

After crossing Africa, 4,300 miles mostly on foot, from 1853 to 1856, drawing detailed maps and discovering the spectacular Victoria Falls, Livingstone returned to Britain to find himself a celebrity festooned with honours. He published his account of his journey under the title "Missionary Travels" and it was an instant best seller. Livingstone used his fame to encourage others to venture into Africa with tales of "God's highway", the great river Zambesi which he believed to be a navigable route to the interior. Amongst his hectic schedule of civic receptions, lectures and royal audiences he gave a brief lecture in December 1856 to the Blantyre Literary and Scientific Institute in the chapel/schoolroom where he had attended as a boy.

Return to the Zambesi

Livingstone was appointed Consul of Quillemane, and returned to Africa in 1858 in charge of a government sponsored expedition to explore the Zambesi. Livingstone had a great liking for his distinctive peaked consul's cap and was depicted wearing it in many of his portraits. He also habitually wore a shirt of "Turkey dyed" cotton (the dye being obtained from the root of the madder plant grown in Turkey), which was made at the Blantyre Cotton Mills until 1873, coincidentally the same year Livingstone died in Africa.

Neither the Zambesi nor the Shire rivers proved to be the highway to the interior which Livingstone had promised. Shifting sandbars, impassable rapids, tropical diseases and Livingstone's own lack of experience in leading Europeans, undermined expedition morale. The project floundered in a catalogue of disagreements, misfortune and loss of life, including that of Livingstone's own wife who died of fever in 1862, only three months after joining him on the Zambesi. In 1863, the British government recalled the expedition, leaving Livingstone's reputation badly tarnished.

Unwilling to leave his steamer, "The Lady Nyassa", in Africa where it would likely fall into the hands of slavers, Livingstone embarked on another amazing venture. With only five days' coal on board, he sailed the shallow drafted river boat for forty five days across the Indian Ocean to Bombay.

When Livingstone returned to Britain he had not seen his children for several years and the youngest, five years old Anna Mary, who had been born at Kuruman, he had never seen at all. However, the reunion was not a happy one for Livingstone. His mother was dying, and shortly after his arrival he heard news that his eldest son Robert had been killed in the American Civil War.

"Dr Livingstone, I presume?"

Despite professional failure and personal tragedy, Livingstone's determination to bring "Christianity and Commerce" to Africa and put an end to the slave trade was not diminished. At that time, the search for the source of the Nile had captured the public imagination and Livingstone was able to raise funds for further exploration. Two years later he was back in Africa without the encumbrance of other Europeans, with a remit from the Royal Geographical Society to explore of the great African watershed and resolve once and for all the debate on the source of the Nile.

By 1871, Livingstone had not been in contact with the outside world for several years. Some efforts had been made to locate him but, apart from occasional reports in the British press that he had been killed by natives, the earlier days of public recognition and media attention had gone. Livingstone might well have faded into obscurity had it not been for "The New York Herald" sending Henry Morton Stanley to "find Livingstone no matter the cost". In a scoop of international proportions and with his greeting of "Dr Livingstone, I presume?" Stanley's journalism rekindled public interest. Portraying Livingstone as a saintly old man heroically struggling on alone to bring civilisation to Africa despite having been abandoned by his own country, Stanley created a myth that was to endure for almost a century and established for Livingstone a place in the annals of history, albeit that it obscured much of the interest and complexity of Livingstone's character and career.

Livingstone had been in pretty bad shape when Stanley arrived at Ujiji. Stanley re-equipped Livingstone with desperately needed supplies and medicines but failed to persuade him to return home to recuperate. When he reluctantly left him after five months of exploring together Stanley would be the last European to see Livingstone alive. For a further two years Livingstone struggled on in appalling conditions and deteriorating health till he died at the isolated village of Ilala on 1st May, 1873, still relentlessly searching for 'the source of the Nile'.

The story of his death and the epic journey of his faithful followers bringing his body 1,500 miles back to the coast to be buried in his native land captured the hearts of Victorian Britain. He was buried in Westminster Abbey with full honours on 18 April, 1877, on a day of national mourning. In the words of Florence Nightingale, he had become "the greatest man of his generation". In Africa that reputation remains to this day and even the most critical of his European biographers have conceded that a certain "greatness" existed in Livingstone.

Livingstone had always been a prolific writer and his diaries and letters reveal that failures weighed heavily on him and that he was severely disappointed that his ideas for Africa had not come to fruition.

75

Ironically, a month after his death, the slave market in Zanzibar was closed and "Christianity and Commerce" began rapidly to penetrate Africa, in what was to become active competition for political expansion and a desperate scramble for colonial domination of the continent.

The Scottish National Memorial to David Livingstone

The Blantyre Cotton Mills went into liquidation in 1904 when imports from India and elsewhere in the British Empire destroyed the cotton spinning industry at home. By 1925, most of the former cotton mill complex had been demolished with the exception of Shuttle Row, the wages office and the building which had previously been David Dale's office. In November, 1925, the Reverend Dr. James MacNair paid a visit to the birthplace of David Livingstone (the "birthroom" was cared for by an old woman who earned a small income from occasional tourists) and was greatly shocked to find that the building was reduced to a slum and scheduled for imminent demolition. Dr. MacNair became determined to renovate the building and establish a memorial to Blantyre's most famous son.

After a pithead meeting with the building's owners, the coalmining firm, William Baird and Company, an appeal was launched to raise the then substantial amount of £12,000 to buy the property and the surrounding grounds and to found a memorial. When the economic recession and uncertain future of the General Strike of 1926 looked like causing the abandonment of the project, an approach to the Sunday Schools of Scotland created a remarkable financial response. Dr. MacNair described how "From city and from glen came streams, often driblets of pennies, that together swelled into a spate so great that it carried us over the bar of our difficulties."

In the end, the appeals target was exceeded, and ninety percent of the total amount had come in the form of small donations from the people of Scotland. The transfer of the property and 9.885 acres of adjacent grounds to the Scottish National Memorial to David Livingstone Trust took place on Whitsunday, 1927, but as negotiations were being finalised a quarrel blew up between William Baird and Company and striking coal miners. The coal miners felled most of the trees around Shuttle Row for firewood believing the land still belonged to the coal owners. However, in clearing the trees, the miners had substantially improved the land for use as a playing field and the

Shuttle Row, David Livingstone Centre, Blantyre

incident brought additional publicity for the plans for the memorial.

Heirlooms and artefacts relating to Livingstone's life, the Blantyre Cotton Mill and the coal mining industry were loaned or donated by local families, societies and Livingstone's descendants. Local schoolchildren and unemployed miners assisted in landscaping the grounds. The Scottish National Memorial to David Livingstone was officially opened on 5th October, 1929, by Her Majesty, Queen Elizabeth, the Queen Mother, then the Duchess of York, who commented that "It seems most appropriate that the birthplace of the great Scotsman should henceforth be a memorial of his achievement as a missionary and pioneer."

Over the decades, the museum and exhibitions have been improved and various features such as the World Fountain, the Africa Pavilion and Jungle Garden added to create at Blantyre a visitor attraction of international repute renamed the David Livingstone Centre.

DAVID LIVINGSTONE

Livingstone reflects on his early life in Blantyre Mills.

Looking back on that life of toil, I cannot but feel thankful that it formed such a material part of my early education: and, were it possible, I should like to begin life over again in the same lowly style and to pass through the same hardy training.

Missionary Travels

UDDINGSTON

David Jamieson

Uddingston owes its name to the Angles who had been politically involved in the area since 700 AD. The first recorded spelling was Odistoun, appearing on the list of landowners giving an oath of fealty to Edward I, and meaning the homestead of Oda, which was a common enough name in northwest Europe. The feminine name Odette is still used in France. Odistoun appears in the Ragman's Roll of 1296, followed swiftly be Evison and later by Udiston.

Early Uddingston

No apology is needed to include Bothwell Castle in the history of Uddingston. It was never in Bothwell Village, and its entrance was from Uddingston. The estate of Bothwell had passed by marriage from David Olifard to Walter de Moravia (or Moray) who it was probably built the castle in the thirteenth century, on a red sandstone promontory overlooking the gorge of the River Clyde. After John Balliol was deposed in 1296, the castle was held on behalf of Edward I of England by Stephen de Brampton until 1289-90 when it was besieged and finally captured by the Scots after a fourteen month blockade. In 1301, following a month long siege, Edward retook the castle with a force of 6,000 men. After the defeat of the English at Bannockburn in 1314, Bothwell Castle was partially dismantled in order that it could not be used as an English base in the future, although it was restored and held for a short time by Edward III until its recapture in 1337 and subsequent second partial demolition. Around 1362, Bothwell Castle was acquired through marriage between Jean Murray and Douglas Archibald, 'the Grim', third Earl of Douglas and Lord of Galloway, and rebuilt on a slightly smaller scale. (Douglas Archibald had earned his nickname from certain unpleasant habits such as keeping a corpse permanently decorating the wall at Threave Castle, the principal seat of the Douglases.) The Black Douglas family forfeited possession of the castle in 1455 and it reverted to the Crown, passing into the possession of the Red Douglas family in 1492. Bothwell Castle was finally abandoned in the seventeenth century and the new Bothwell Castle built in the then fashionable Palladian style by Archibald

Douglas, using some stone from the old castle. Bothwell Castle Mansion House eventually fell into a state of disrepair and, no longer needed by the Earl of Home, was pulled down in 1930.

Under the patronage of the Douglases, the farmers of Uddingston would have had a peaceful existence. The farmers, or portioners, held their land from Lord Douglas and, subject to his prior right, had to grind their corn at the prescribed mill. They would use the Calder Water Mill along what is now Old Mill Road and, in later years, the new Calder Mill, now also in ruins, at Broomhouse beside the present day Zoo.

We know the names of these vassals because they failed in their duty to supply wax to the tombs of St Mungo and his mother in Glasgow, an omission recorded in the Cathedral records of 1496. Their names, with spellings modernised, were Caldwell, Scott, Wilkinson, Pettigrew, Jack, Braidwood, Silverton, Wilson and Crosby. These men of "Odingstoun" were threatened with excommunication "by bell, book and candle". It is interesting to note that some of these families continued to hold land in the village until recent times.

Uddingston itself had a chapel at Meadowbank. The site is near the river and is now covered by the railway embankment. There is no existing picture or description of it. The chapel was dedicated to St Molaise, an Irish Saint who was a disciple of St Columba. Title deeds of property in the vicinity show Chapelflats, Chapelacre, Chapelcroft and Chapelhaugh. The site of Gardenside Street was once called Crucisvale.

In medieval Uddingston, the only road worthy of the name was the Glasgow Road, which originally went through the Policies (or Castle Grounds) and then more or less on the line of Old Glasgow Road along by the river and on by a bridge over the Calder near where it met the Clyde. It carried a growing number of ox-carts and panniers after the Bothwell Bridge was built early in the fifteenth century.

The land was cultivated on the run-rig system, the ridges being shared among five or six landowners who held the land subject to their use of the mill and a joint right of the Muir for their livestock. The Muir of Muirmadzean stretched beyond what was later to be Bellshill. We know that in the right season of the year it was covered by the flowers of the broom. The Muir left its name on Muiredge, Laighmuir and Gallamuir, an abbreviation of the Gallowmuir where hangings took place, southeast of the Cross.

Eighteenth Century Uddingston

The oldest inhabited house in the village is Knowehead Cottage, built in 1629, which was used as an inn. The land on Knowehead estate had been granted by the Earl of Angus (a member of the Douglas family) to the Wilkie family in 1629. A future laird of Knowehead House was General Wilkie who was to command troops in the Crimean War and whose name is commemorated by the present day street, General's Gate. Only one gate post of the original General's gate remains and Knowehead House was demolished in 1968. The two oldest inns are the Rowantree and the Plough, now called the Anvil.

In 1745, Prince Charles' army marched back through the village and there is a local story that the farmer in Glasgow Road covered his horses' heads to save them from being commandeered. After 1745, there were increasingly peaceful conditions in the United Kingdom, and before the end of the eighteenth century, tourists were coming from England into Scotland. The era of the turnpike roads, the tolls and the stage coach had begun. The first stage coach ran from London to Glasgow in 1790. There was a stage coach change at the back of the main street. Old Glasgow Road, and later the present Glasgow Road, would resound to the call of the coach-horn.

In the more settled times that followed the '45 rebellion, several larger houses were built, including Birkenshaw House in 1782 (now Easter Farm), Clydeside House, Fallside House, Viewpark House, Thornwood House and Meadowbank House.

The main road no longer went through the Castle Grounds and the roads improved until the Hamilton-Glasgow road was built about 1825. Around the same time, Thomas Telford built the bridge over the Calder, which lasted until after the tram-cars.

In the first half of the eighteenth century, sixty families were recorded in the village and by 1795, there was a population of 287, including the out-farms. Apart from those living in the scattered farms, the population would have lived in the "old toun" or in the Croft area by Croftbank Farm. There were several cottages at Croftbank dating from the seventeenth century which became nicknamed "Wee Ireland" in the early nineteenth century after immigrant families had moved in. The cottages would have had earthen floors and walls of clay and rubble with tree trunks for roof beams and roofs of thatch. Many of the cottages had small annexes used as weaving sheds. A larger building with more than one loom stood almost opposite Easter Farm and was not demolished until the 1960s.

In the eighteenth century lint, otherwise known as flax, was grown in fields to the east of the village, and a tenement row, demolished in 1971, was called Lindams, a corruption of Lint Dams, built on the site of the shallow pools formed for soaking the lint fibres. This was called retting the lint, which produced a pervading smell like the stale water from a flower vase. In the mid eighteenth century, the government invited thread manufacturers to enter into a competition for "bounties" for producing the best thread made in Scotland from home grown flax. The Misses Leslie of Uddingston produced the best thread in the district and accordingly, entered the contest in 1763. Despite winning the competition, they did not receive the promised awards. They were passed over in some mysterious way and it was hinted that there had been dirty work behind the scenes, despite the prestigious support of the Duchess of Hamilton, the local member of parliament, a local minister and others. A pair of ruffles made from the Misses Leslie's thread was presented to His Majesty George III "which he did not disdain to wear." The incident was reported at length in "The Hamilton Advertiser" in 1940, when the government was again encouraging the production of home grown flax.

Like many other places locally, many villagers engaged at their homes in handloom weaving which went on from about the seventeenth century for two hundred years. The necessary material for weaving was supplied to the villagers and the finished cloth collected from them. Although relatively well paid, the weavers, during periods of unemployment, set about other jobs such as building the high walls round the Castle Policies or helping with stone quarries in the district. The large modern mills at Blantyre and Bellshill eventually took away their trade.

Victorian Uddingston

Uddingston in the main was built in the Victorian age. It was then that almost all the tenements and most of the large houses were erected. The latter was the result of increasing prosperity, improved communications and the general amenity of Uddingston. The first such development was Douglas Gardens which was begun around 1868. Gardenside Avenue was commenced in 1871. A fine house, nicknamed "Candyman's Castle", was built in 1857 by John Poynter, a wealthy chemical manufacturer in Glasgow. Its actual name was Clydeneuk

House. Its owner had begun business in a small way with a cart collecting rags and bones, in exchange for which he handed out sweets to children. The house was demolished around 1956. The Red Brig, a red sandstone bridge over the Clyde at Greyfriars, was built in 1840. Kyle Park was laid out in 1882, where Bronze Age incinery urns were unearthed when the roads were being made. The Main Street and Glasgow Road had the notable distinction of being totally Victorian (with the exception of Loanhead Mansions) and were built of local red sandstone.

As you will see from the detailed Ordnance Survey map of 1855, Uddingston was a great place for wells – Jacob's Well, Springwell, Wellbank, Docken Well and so on. Many of the larger houses built before 1878 had their own pumps or wells. Gravitation or piped water arrived in 1880.

Why was the development of Uddingston, which had a start over some neighbouring places, overtaken by towns such as Bellshill and Motherwell? Certainly, in the second half of the nineteenth century, the population grew dramatically from around 1,400 in 1866 to 7,500 in 1899, but building virtually ceased in 1900 and did not start again until 1960s. One reason was that space was constricted by the River Clyde, and also the presence of sand at the centre of the village was not an ideal foundation for heavy machinery. As coal began to be worked in a ring of collieries round the village, there was also a risk of subsidence.

Newcomers to Uddingston may not realise that fifty years ago the village was surrounded by collieries and you could not walk far without reaching one. The official name of Bellshill Road is the Coal Highway as coal used to come that way in carts to be collected for Glasgow. Uddingston had only one colliery actually in the village, Hendrie's pit at Maryville at the back of what is now the Roman Catholic Church, and which was abandoned in 1883. There are seventeen feet of coal under the village, but it is unlikely that this will ever be worked, for it would be uneconomic to extract and drainage is likely to present problems. Although the amenity of the district has improved by the passing of the mining era, many Uddingstonians are none the worse of mining blood in their veins. I like to believe that the grandfathers have passed on to their descendants some of the courage and good humour and the willingness to help a neighbour which was so much a part of the old mining tradition.

Uddingston first gained a reputation for the manufacture of agricultural implements from John Wilkie (1770-1829) and his son James (1802-1849). The family lived in Crofthead House, which was only pulled down after the last War. From 1850 George Gray carried on making Wilkie's Ploughs at the Kiln. The Big Foundry was in Crofthead Street next to the showground. It later became the Victoria Theatre, a music hall. Goldie's Wee Foundry was in Old Mill Road, next to Gallamuir House. James Hornal, a blacksmith, made agricultural machinery at Hornal's Engineering Works, in what was to become Crofthead Street. John Gray's Uddingston Ironworks made machinery across the railway. It finished up at the turn of the century, and its office became the Caley Bowling Club.

The railway reached Uddingston from Glasgow in 1849 and the Edinburgh branch in 1869. From 1878, the North British Line had two stations – three if you count Maryville, which closed in 1907 as a result of competition from the Glasgow trams. The North British Line closed in 1955. The Glasgow trams ran from 1907 to 1948 and the Lanarkshire trams from 1909 to 1931. The motorway arrived in 1968.

Up to the middle of the last century there were scarcely any shops in a village such as Uddingston. Communities were more self supporting. The first merchants we know of were Merchant Eglinton and Andrew Jack whose names are recorded in McPherson's Directory of 1862. They were both in the Old Town. The Co-operative Society was founded in 1861. Its first shop was at Greenrig Street, a single storey building, at the corner of Croftbank Street. The premises were later moved to Old Mill Road. If you look at the Uddingston Directory of 1862 you will note several shopkeepers, and in the twenty years that followed, there were many more. Nowadays there is a large superstore.

With an increase in population, provision had to be made for places of worship. The first was the United Presbyterian Church in 1863, then the Free Church in 1877 and the Congregational Church in 1880. The Free Church was renamed the Chalmers United Free Church in 1900, after Dr Chalmers, one of the greatest orators of his day. The pits brought in a large number of Roman Catholics, mainly from County Donegal, and they opened a combined chapel and school in 1883, moving to a separate church in 1902. St Andrew's Scottish Episcopal Church opened in 1890. We have a Church of the Nazarene and a Baptist Church together with two Brethren meeting houses. For a few years after the last War, Clydeside House was occupied by two or three monks. In 1983 the Free Church combined with Trinity Church which takes the name of Uddingston Old Parish Church. Chalmers Church was demolished in 1983.

Uddingston's first school was a room in a tenement property at the back of Main Street in Old Mill Road in 1825. The fees were a shilling a month, without writing, one shilling and two pence with writing, and one shilling and four pence, with grammar.

The Free Church built a school in 1844, and the Church of Scotland then built one, eighteen feet away. The Free Church School flourished under Dominie Smith, despite Lady Douglas threatening dismissal to any of her employees who did not send their children to the parish school. Pupils arrived from Bothwell, Blantyre, Broomhouse and Bellshill to such an extent that it took over the Church of Scotland school, and when the Grammar School was opened in 1885 next to the Station, Dominie Smith was appointed the first rector and continued there until his retiral in 1890. Extensions were made to Uddingston Grammar School around 1961 and again in 1994. Uddingston Academy in Church Street was a boarding school.

Few people realise that Uddingston had a football team which once played senior teams at Meadowbank (not the present school fields). They drew a game with the Glasgow Rangers and, what is more, also drew at Ibrox. Money talked in those days and Rangers signed John Hendry, the Uddingston defender, who was reported to have been the best man on the field. About 1889 Uddingston were playing Royal Albert (Larkhall), Clyde, Falkirk, Hibernians, Albion Rovers, Hamilton Academicals. . . . .

It was Uddingston Cricket Club that put the name of the village on the map, and its achievements were remarkable for a place of its size. Founded in 1882, the first fifty years of the club were recorded by James S. McGill and the centenary by Robert McFarlane, perhaps the last of the Uddingston "greats". It is hard to believe that our village has played English County sides. For example, we met Gloucestershire in a two-day game in 1902 in which the legendary Jessop scored 141 in the second innings. The general opinion has been that our best professional was A. Broadbent (Yorkshire) and our best amateur, A. C. Cullen. Attendances topped 2,000 in the old days. Today, local cricket does not count as a spectator sport.

As the years passed the cricket pitch gradually tilted to the south as a result of mining subsidence. The pavilion required shoring up

Gow's Corner, Uddingston

Trams at Uddingston Cross

and, as Sheriff Dobie used to say at Committee meetings, it was like being in a ship going down stern first. As the result of successful litigation, the National Coal Board settled out of court.

Archibald Tunnock died in 1981. It is unlikely there will ever be a more remarkable Uddingstonian. He built an enormous business without borrowing. His caramel wafers have gone round the globe. Mr Tunnock wrote all the firm's catchy advertisements himself. Once, when an advertising expert rewrote some of Archie's copy, Archie said "You've corrected my grammar and polished everything up. But when folks read it they'll say, 'That's no' Archie Tunnock!' Just put it back the way I wrote it. They'll have a laugh. But I'll have the last laugh. I'll sell more biscuits!"

The sole son of a local baker, Thomas Tunnock, he only went into the business to help his mother after his father's death. He built up a catering business, running a new bakery and shop and later a tea-room in Main Street. From there after the last War, he opened in stages a large factory, which is still run as a family business by his two sons.

Near the end of the century, Uddingston had a hotel, the Royal Hotel, but in 1885 it lost its Sunday licence on account of drunkenness among its clientele. It had been built at a cost of £12,000. (It should be explained that, until 1977, drink could only be sold in Scotland on a Sunday at bars and hotels to "bona fide" travellers, so a Sunday licence could make a hotel very popular!) After a fire, an earlier hotel in Main Street was split up into dwelling houses. Since then we have had two hotels and numerous restaurants including Italian, Chinese and Indian. We have had two picture houses which did not survive television.

Present Day Uddingston

We have a good District Planning Department, and they are much to be commended for consulting the public so well about the Local Plan. Lanark County Council's Uddingston Town Map had proposed totally to redevelop the village's commercial centre and make radical changes to the road pattern. In the preparation of the Local Plan, however, Hamilton District Council reviewed these proposals and the resultant document retained virtually all the existing physical fabric of the village centre. Even proposals for the demolition of Hawthornlee and Lincluden were successfully campaigned against by the Ratepayers Committee and the properties still stand in Main Street, housing the

Bank of Scotland and two adjacent shops. Modern developments have been built in the Castle Policies but the ancient trees have been carefully preserved. The people of Uddingston now have two new football pitches and a footbridge over the River Clyde. The river is gradually becoming cleaner as evidenced by herons, cormorants and goosanders.

With the designation of Bothwellpark Industrial Estate in 1991 as an Industrial Improvement Area, financial assistance has become available to help local companies in the upgrading of their premises, and employment opportunities in and adjacent to Uddingston have improved. The main employers on the Estate are United Artists, Alexandra Workwear, and Dawnfresh Seafoods Limited, a seafood processing plant which opened there in 1993. The domestic appliance factory, Creda Airdun, closed in 1990 and, amidst considerable opposition from local residents and shopkeepers, its former site at Bothwell Road was acquired by Safeway for the erection of a Presto superstore.

The Community Council is active and has maintained our annual gala day when most others have faded out. We can look forward with hope to the new century.

BOTHWELL CASTLE

When he was a guest at the New Bothwell Castle, Sir Walter Scott wrote "Young Lochinvar", and also the following fragment of a ballad. "Pembroke's ruined towers" refers to the grant, by Edward I, in 1301 of Bothwell Castle to Aymer de Valence, Earl of Pembroke and Warden of Scotland, following the castle's capture by the English.

"When fruitful Clydesdale's apple bowers
Are mellowing in the noon;
When sighs round Pembroke's ruined towers
The sultry breath of June:
If chance by Bothwell's lovely braes
A wanderer thou hast been,
Or hid thee from the summer's blaze
In Blantyre's bowers of green.
Full where the copsewood opens wild,
Thy pilgrim step hath staid,
Where Bothwell's towers in ruins piled,
O'erlook the verdant glade."

Sir Walter Scott

Old and New Castles, Bothwell

BOTHWELL

Russell Thomson

Introduction

Named after its location on a promontory above the River Clyde, "Bothwell" is derived from the Celtic for either "a habitation by the river" or "a castle upon an imminence". The village lies on the north east boundary of the Clyde, covering an area of some five square miles, and has a population of 6,179.

Early Bothwell

Ask any stranger what he knows about Bothwell, and you can be almost certain that he will mention the Castle. Beautifully situated on the Clyde, it is probably the finest thirteenth century castle existing in Scotland today. It is only natural, therefore, to assume that the village of Bothwell began with the building of this great Norman structure. This is not the case. The main approach of the castle comes from Uddingston, and the building is discussed in more detail in the chapter on that village.

The Olifard family owned the Bothwell Estate in the first half of the thirteenth century. It is probable that they had a house somewhere in Bothwell and the site of the present Manse is a likely location. The land subsequently passed to Walter De Moravia (or Moray) who founded Bothwell Castle in the second half of the century. His tombstone, carrying the Moray Arms, lies in Bothwell Parish Church. During the fourteenth century, Bothwell Castle changed hands several times between the Scots and the English. Archibald "The Grim", Third Earl of Douglas, acquired the Barony of Bothwell in 1362 and restored the Castle but it was forfeited by his family in 1455 and reverted to the Crown, passing into the possession of the Red Douglas family in 1492. In 1669 and using stonework from Bothwell Castle, Archibald Douglas, First Earl of Forfar, erected a Palladian style mansion in the Castle grounds and Bothwell Castle Mansion House stood until 1930 when it was demolished. Overlooking the motorway at the Raith roundabout stands Bothwell Park House, originally built in 1750 as the Dower house of the Mansion. One of the Adams brothers may have designed the house, for it shows some evidence of the Adams' style, although

Robert, the most famous of the brothers, was only a student at the time of the building and could not have been its architect.

Archibald the Grim was also responsible for the erection of the Collegiate Church of St Bride on the foundations of a twelfth century Norman church which itself had been erected on an early Celtic sacred site. The church was built in 1398 and its choir dedicated to St Bride, the patron saint of the Black Douglas family. The design of the church reflects the fact that by the turn of the fifteenth century, the Gothic style of architecture had replaced the Norman as a more functional and economical way to construct a large building. St Bride's Church has the stone barrel vaults of the early Gothic style, typical of many of Scotland's old churches because there was little wood in the country and an abundance of stone. It makes an impressive ceiling.

We may also have to thank Archibald the Grim for Bothwell Bridge, since he might have founded the original bridge, the only structure then spanning the Clyde between the river's source and Glasgow. It had five arches, with a twelve foot wide causeway, rising steeply up to the central gate house where the tolls were collected.

The Covenanters
The history of the Covenanters in Hamilton District has its own chapter in this book, but it is appropriate to mention here the monument erected in 1903 at Bothwell Bridge to commemorate the battle which took place on 22 June, 1679, between the troops of Charles II and the Covenanters. Four hundred Covenanters were killed and another twelve hundred taken prisoner.

Agriculture
From the fourteenth to the nineteenth century, agriculture was the main occupation of the people of the village. The soil in the area was superior to that in the rest of Bothwell Parish and accounted for the early establishment of the prosperity of Bothwell and Uddingston. The discovery of lime in the eighteenth century greatly increased the yield of the land. The weather in Bothwell was also a help to the farmer, described by one contemporary writer as being "peculiarly salubrious". Neighbouring Uddingston eventually became a centre for engineering but the advantages and disadvantages of the early industrial revolution bypassed rural Bothwell.

Weaving

At the end of the eighteenth century Bothwell's population was 425, including the Castle and out-farms. Along Main Street and Green Street were the weavers' cottages. Bothwell weavers were known as contract labourers. The raw materials were brought in from Glasgow by city merchants who then collected and paid for the woven material.

The opening of Bothwell Mill rang the death knell of the home weavers. It was built at Waterside on the Clyde and operated ninety power looms. In its turn, it disappeared without trace as more economic mills such as Blantyre Mill, with better equipment, commandeered the market. Some of the unemployed Bothwell weavers went across the Clyde to Blantyre Mill to work whilst others were given employment building the walls round the Castle policies to avoid the poverty created by the decline of handloom weaving as a major trade. In 1852, more of the Bothwell weavers were able to cross the river on the suspension toll bridge to work in the new Blantyre Mill or turkey red factory.

The Clyde paid the price of this industrial development, and the once plentiful stocks of salmon were decimated by the discharges from the dyeworks on the banks, by pollution leaching into the river from nearby factories and by the constant traffic of steamboats. A dam was built in the 1780s between Blantyre Mill and Bothwell which prevented the salmon from swimming upriver in the spawning season. By the end of the nineteenth century, however, the worsening pollution of the river, exacerbated by the new mining industry of Lanarkshire, caused the closure of the mills, and two hundred Blantyre workers were to cross the bridge to earn their daily bread in Bothwell. Blantyre Bridge was demolished in 1949.

The Impact of Glasgow

With the coming of the industrial revolution to central Scotland, Bothwell began to be viewed by the wealthier citizens of Glasgow as a quiet haven to escape from the crowded bustle of the smoky city, whether for holidays or for more permanent residence. The business men made their money from tobacco, molasses and other manufactured goods and Glasgow grew to be the second biggest city in the empire. Bothwell became a very desirable village in which to build a house. It had many natural advantages for the wealthy Glaswegian, being on the main Glasgow Carlisle coach route or better still, reached conveniently from Blantyre which had a regular passenger train service. Later, the service was further improved by the opening by the Caledonian Railway Company of a passenger station in 1877 on Main Street opposite the Clyde Hotel, and the opening in 1878 by the Glasgow, Bothwell, Hamilton and Coatbridge Railway Company of the North British Line which included a station on Station Road. There were also tram lines between Bothwell and Glasgow. The village had recognised links with antiquity in its thirteenth century castle and with the nobility who lived in the adjacent seventeenth century mansion house. There was plenty of arable land available for building. Below the top soil of Bothwell village lay a vast quantity of red sandstone, and quarrying near the river was easy and the labour cheap. It was to these early Glasgow business and professional men, who used Bothwell as their country dormitory, that we owe much of the village's environmental charm today. Not only did they build fine houses but they surrounded them with expansive gardens, retained existing mature trees and planted more. New roads, crescents and churches appeared on the map and the village began to develop the pattern which it still retains today.

In addition to the permanent residents, in summertime Bothwell welcomed an influx of holiday visitors. In 1840, one writer had described how doctors in Glasgow were advising patients in a delicate state of health to seek convalescence in Bothwell village on account of the healthy climate. The Clyde Hotel, now the Bothwell Bridge Hotel, opened in 1860 to cater for visitors. The Douglas Arms Inn had such a reputation for cleanliness and hospitality it became known as Cleanly Meg's, a complimentary title for the owner, Meg Steel. Meg can still be seen, her image carved at the termination of a hood mould of the nave window in the parish church, among other Bothwell characters.

Coal Mining

Just as it was getting into its stride as a residential village, a great discovery was made by geologists which was to annoy the residents of Bothwell. Below the red sandstone were rich deposits of coal. This discovery was made in the middle of the nineteenth century and was to transform the life of the village over the next sixty years. In 1878, the North British Railway linked Bothwell Castle Colliery with Glasgow, and mining commenced in earnest. To span the Clyde and connect Bothwell with Blantyre and Hamilton, a magnificent viaduct

95

bridge was built at the same time. The population of 471 at the end of the eighteenth century jumped to 3,097 at the end of the nineteenth. Miners came from all over Scotland and Ireland to work in the pits. Some found accommodation in Bothwell. In 1898, the pit owners, Baird and Sons Limited, built a special block of tenements called the Castle Square to house their workers. It was immediately nicknamed the Jubilee since it was opened on the 50th anniversary of Queen Victoria's accession to the throne. Next to Castle Square was Waverley Place, also built to house miners. Both developments were demolished during the late 1960s and early 1970s, and sheltered housing built on the site.

Schools

With the opening of the pits, fine new stone buildings were constructed to accommodate the increase in the school population. The Protestant primary school on Hamilton Road was built in 1887 and for a while housed the infant department of Bothwell Primary School. This is now contained within the new school. The Roman Catholic school was built in 1909 and was also intended to serve miners' children from the neighbouring community of Bothwellhaugh. This school, however, was never popular with Bothwell parents and when, in 1937, there was danger of subsidence, it was closed down and removed in 1942 to Bothwellhaugh. St Bride's Roman Catholic school opened in 1973.

Elmwood Secondary School opened in 1872. Run by Franciscan nuns, it was primarily a private boarding school for young ladies. In 1918, the school was officially recognised by the Scottish Education Department for grant aid, and started to accept a number of day girls for schooling to certificate standards. The school closed in 1977 and the property was converted into flats. Private sheltered accommodation was built in the grounds and opened in 1983. It was the first development of its kind in Scotland.

Bothwellhaugh

Bothwellhaugh was formerly a dairy farming community approximately two miles from Bothwell Village. Its earlier claim to fame had been that the assassination, in 1570, of Regent Moray had been perpetrated by James Hamilton of Bothwellhaugh. Following the discovery of the rich coal seams round Hamilton and Bothwell, the Bent Colliery Company Limited, which already worked three pits in the Hamilton area, took out the lease of mineral rights at Bothwellhaugh. The first pit of the Hamilton Palace Colliery was sunk in 1884 and formally opened the same year. The second pit was prepared some time during the following two years. To house their workers, the mine owners erected a "village" of colliery rows close to the pithead which was also known as the Pallis. The first phase of the development was completed by the early 1890s and the second by 1905. The properties ranged from single rooms to three-apartment houses and were, in the main, better quality than those built in neighbouring mining towns.

Peak production of coal was reached in 1913 when an average of 2,000 tons per day of high quality coal was being extracted. Both pits continued to be worked until the 1950s, at which time the colliery was declared uneconomic and was finally closed in 1959. By 1965, the last of the villagers had left Bothwellhaugh and the houses were demolished. The area was incorporated into Strathclyde Park in the early 1970s.

Churches

By the early nineteenth century, St Bride's Church had fallen into a state of disrepair and was abandoned as a place of worship in 1828. In 1833, however, the architect David Hamilton built the new Parish Church of Bothwell, to the west of the Collegiate Church and forming its nave. The building was further restored in 1898 and, in 1933, the old and the new churches, which until then had stood separately on different levels, were brought together as a single unit. By the entrance to the church grounds stands the memorial to Joanna Baillie, born in Bothwell Manse in 1762 and an eminent poetess and playwright, and friend to Sir Walter Scott. Her memorial contains beautiful examples of nineteenth century Italian mosaics.

Nearby stands the Russell Memorial Hall. In 1891 Archibald Russell of Auchinraith bought the former school house on the site in order to prevent the erection of tenement buildings which would overlook the church and the churchyard. The ground was gifted to the Bothwell Parish Church in 1904 and, in 1906, Archibald Russell's widow had the church hall erected in her husband's memory and endowed with an annual sum for its upkeep.

Kirkfield Church was built in 1860, a time when the decline of the home weaving trade was resulting in extreme poverty among the

St Bride's Kirk,
Bothwell

villagers. While the church was being built, the Kirkfield members worshipped in a school in Uddingston in the morning, or in the afternoon at Wooddean Church which had been erected seven years earlier. The two churches were amalgamated in 1941, and united with St Bride's in 1976, to become Bothwell Parish Church. Kirkfield and Wooddean Church was demolished in 1984 and flats built on the site.

In 1916, the Society of Jesus opened Craighead Retreat House on Whistleberry Road, just outside Bothwell. St Bride's Roman Catholic Church was opened in 1973 in Fallside Road, before which time the Roman Catholic community had worshipped in the Miners' Welfare. The Poor Clares moved into a convent attached to the church.

The Bothwell Evangelical Church, formerly known as the Asher Hall, is located in the old Parochial Chambers. The building was extended in 1993 and, in 1994, won a Royal Institute of British Architecture Regional Award.

Community Life

Victorian Bothwell had a Bowling Green and a Horticultural Society, both opened in 1868, and a Public Subscription Library which started in 1876. The Public Halls opened in May 1888. The Bothwell Directory of 1890 records the Bothwell Lawn Tennis Club, Curling Club, Literary Society, Choral Society and Burns Club.

Mr James Donald, a prominent chemical manufacturer in Glasgow, left a bequest of £3,000 to the village and the Donald Institute, a suite of recreation rooms for billiards, whist or dominoes, was built in 1910 and run on strictly temperance principles. The building now houses the public library.

Kirklands Hospital was founded in 1871. Extensively rebuilt in 1990, it is now a flagship in the field of care for people with a mental handicap.

Bothwell Castle Golf Course opened in 1923 on land within the Castle Policies given to the community by the Earl of Home.

Post-War Bothwell

The 1914-18 War caused a heavy death toll in the village, and nearly every family was affected. A war memorial was unveiled in 1923 on Bothwell Main Street.

The Woodlands scheme, commenced in 1919, was partly the outcome of the political "homes for heroes" slogan, and also the first county council housing estate to be constructed in Bothwell. Wooddean estate followed in 1924. It was built during the economic depression and a section of the scheme was allocated to the unemployed.

The changes which took place in the village between the two World Wars largely resulted from better communications with Glasgow and other parts of Lanarkshire. The public hall was in regular use for political meetings, socials and dances. The annual flower show became a notable date in the county calendar. A thriving public interest committee was active in the affairs of the village. The motor car and the Second World War were to play a large part in altering the image of Bothwell as a quiet country village. One of Bothwell's unique links with its clean residential image disappeared during the 1939-45 War. The underground tunnel which had allowed the miners to pass below the Main Street to their homes in the Castle Square was bricked up as an air raid shelter. The Miners' Welfare, famous for billiards and Saturday night dances as well as political and trade union meetings, was sold to the Catholic Diocese in 1956 as a place of worship, and demolished in 1992. The public hall, once the centre of village life, was demolished in 1971. Large residential mansions were divided into flats as their original owners died, left the district or found the cost of maintaining them uneconomic. Braidenhill House, one of Bothwell's largest homes, became the Silvertrees Hotel. Fairfield House has become a retirement home. Elmwood Mansion and Haxton House have been divided into flats. Wooddean was converted into a children's home in 1946 and run as a home until 1966 when the children were moved to Blantyre.

Other changes were taking place. Bothwell Castle Colliery was nationalised by the Labour Government in 1946. It had been estimated that coal supplies would last until 1963 but flooding and the collapse of a shaft brought about the closure by the National Coal Board in 1950. The viaduct was dismembered and the LMS and LNE stations closed respectively in 1950 and 1951. The LMS railway company left an ugly eyesore in the centre of the village. It was fortunate that, in Tom Coughtrie of Fairfield Lodge, Bothwell had a resident with vision and determination. In 1956, he bought the old station for the Belmos Engineering Company which he had founded in Bellshill, and converted the old station into a modern light engineering factory which opened in 1957. Furthermore, he insisted that his company's architect landscape the site so that his factory harmonised with the church of St

Bride's and the adjacent sand-stone buildings. Tom Coughtrie became Lanarkshire's first conservationist and environmentalist before these terms became the fashionable words that they are today. The factory not only brought new economic vitality into the village, it brought a new heart as well.

The 1960s and 1970s saw the death of Bothwell's traditional industries. In the early 1900s there had been seven farms in production but today not one is left. Market gardening, too, has vanished, with the last tomato nursery, at Bothwell Bank House, closing in the late 1970s. Around the same time the Cottage Bakery closed and the Waterside ceased fruit growing. Today, employment in Bothwell is mainly service based, in hotels, food retailing and shops, and 62.8% of the population work outside the village.

Shopping patterns, too, have changed. By the mid 1960s, the only pre-war shops remaining were the Co-op, Tunnocks and Luigi Arbascelli's Cafe. All have now gone, the last of these to close being Tunnocks in 1994. The only remaining pre-war business remaining is Flemings the Joiners. Two small independent craftsmen, Gilchrist the Jewellers and Mackay the Gunsmiths, opened respectively in the mid 1970s and in 1980 and there are a few distribution warehouses on the outskirts of the village.

The opening of the M74 in 1968 removed the heavy traffic which thundered through the village, but also opened up the possibility of Bothwell joining the commuter belt for Glasgow. Between 1971 and 1991, the population increased from 3,800 to 6,179. In 1964, large scale local authority house building had commenced in Fallside Road, and from the 1970s onwards there was extensive private house building in the Bothwell Castle Policies and on smaller sites throughout the village. With a growing awareness of the need to preserve the village, a series of initiatives was introduced resulting in the designation of the town centre as a Conservation Area and in the Main Street Improvement Scheme of 1973. The Bothwell Village Association was formed in October, 1973. The late Councillor Terry Grieve played a large part in the upgrading of Bothwell Village. Improvement to the village centre continues, and Griqua Terrace was cleaned and upgraded in 1992.

Bothwell has a well-established link with Jouy-en-Josas in northern France, and a twinning charter between the two communities was signed in 1977. Bothwell received the Royal Mail International Twinning Award in 1993.

Large parts of the banks of the Clyde at Bothwell Castle have been designated as Sites of Special Scientific Interest. The Clyde Walkway runs through Bothwell from the memorial footbridge to Bothwell Castle and on to Uddingston. There is still just enough natural countryside in Bothwell to provide the correct balance between man and his environment. The church and its grounds, the Castle, the parks, the bowling green and the golf course must be retained at all costs. The Clyde with its delightful riverside walks offer new possibilities to villagers who care about Bothwell village.

BOTHWELL BANK

The First Statistical Account (1791) records how an English gentleman travelling in Palestine encountered a Scots woman sitting with her baby at the door of her house and singing "Bothwell Bank, thou bloomest fair". She introduced the traveller as a relative to her husband, an officer in the Turkish army, and he was lavishly entertained in their household. The writer goes on to record that the estates of Sweethope and Bothwell Park now occupied a good part of Bothwell Banks.

On the blythe beltane, as I went,
Be mysel attour the green bent,
Wharby the crystal waves of Clyde
Throch saughs and hanging hazels glyde,
There sadly sitting on a brae,
I heard a damsel speak her wae.

"O Bothwell bank, thou blumest fair,
But ah! thou mak'st my heart fou sair!
For a' beneath thy holts sae grene
My luve and I wad sit at ene;
While, primroses and daisies mixt
Wi' bluebells, in my locks he fixt.

But he left me ae drearie day,
And haplie now sleeps in the clay;
Without ae sich his dethe to roun,
Without ae flouir his grave to croun!
O Bothwell bank, thou blumest fair,
But ah! thou mak'st my heart fou sair!"

Anon

The Very Reverend Doctor Hugh Wylie & The Lord Lieutenant of Lanarkshire, Hutchison B. Sneddon unveiling the memorial panel in the Parish churchyard

HAMILTON AND THE COVENANTING TRADITION

William M. Niven

"Blows the wind today and the sun and the rain are flying!
Blows the wind on the moors today and now
Where above the graves of the martyrs the whaups are crying
My heart remembers how."

Robert Louis Stevenson

The Covenanting period in Scottish history covered a period of fifty years, from 1638 – 1688, during the seventeenth century. The Reformation in 1560 had established the Presbyterian faith firmly in Scotland but when Charles I came to the throne in 1625 he proved to be headstrong and unwilling to heed his royal advisers.

The Covenanting movement arose through the imposition on the Scottish nation of Episcopacy and the appointment of bishops. Charles wished to impose religious uniformity on England and Scotland. Riots took place in July, 1637, and the nobility, lairds and the Church of Scotland came together in February, 1638, to sign the National Covenant in Greyfriars Church, Edinburgh. These Covenanters swore loyalty to the Crown but pledged themselves to support the Presbyterian form of worship. This bulwark of faith was further demonstrated by the ratification of the Solemn League and Covenant in 1643.

By this juncture, however, civil war had broken out in England between the parliamentarian Roundheads and the Cavaliers who fought on the side of the Crown. From 1645, when James Nasmyth was appointed as a minister of the Old Parish Church of Hamilton, it can be fairly stated that, in one way and another, Hamilton and its people were to play centre stage on many occasions in the next forty three years.

Nasmyth's sympathies lay very strongly on the side of the Covenanters, as did those of many members of his congregation. The first Duke of Hamilton held devout Episcopalian views and commanded a Scottish army who were defeated by the forces of Oliver Cromwell to whom the power in the kingdom had passed. James

Nasmyth preached a famous sermon on the Sunday, in the presence of the Duke of Hamilton, before setting out for Preston. It is said that Nasmyth denounced the Duke with the following words – "Behold him, behold him, for you will never see his face again". This prophecy became all too true. The English army at Preston proved superior and the Duke was taken prisoner. He was beheaded at Whitehall in 1649 shortly before the execution of Charles I.

After the execution of Charles I, the Commonwealth under Cromwell began. The Scottish nation, in another twist, proclaimed the late king's son as Charles II, brought the new king over from the continent and put their trust in his promises to provide a framework for the Presbyterian faith. Cromwell's army came north and defeated the Scots at Dunbar. English troops were left as garrisons at various locations, including Hamilton where Colonel Lambert and his men were attacked by Covenanters under Colonel Ker. The English beat the Covenanters off in a running fight at Cadzow Bridge, Hamilton, which became known as the Battle of Hieton. The forces of Cromwell established a garrison in the town and the Parish Church records state in October 1650 "This dayes was no session keepit, because the enemie was in the Kingdom." The following year, the second Duke of Hamilton died of wounds received during Charles II's defeat at the battle of Worcester.

James Nasmyth continued to adopt a strong Covenanting posture and fulminated in the pulpit against Cromwell's regime. His capacity to survive arrest and imprisonment over the years of his ministry continues to be a source of wonder when his bitter denunciation of authority is considered.

In the year 1660, Charles II was proclaimed King and the monarchy restored. It should be remembered that Scotland and England were still separate kingdoms linked through a single monarch. Charles had the opportunity to establish peace and good order in Scotland but instead he pursued a tragic strategy of breaking his promises to the Scottish nation and ejecting four hundred ministers who refused to comply with the Episcopal laws. Thirteen of fourteen ministers in Hamilton Presbytery were 'outed' or ejected, and twelve more in Lanark Presbytery. Thus began the famous conventicles, or field meetings, where rebellious ministers and their congregations worshipped in the open air. The Crown used force to suppress the dissension and large fines were exacted. The catalyst was the Battle of

Rullion Green in 1666 where General Dalziel and his dragoons overwhelmed the Covenanting forces. This battle began the First Resistance and in Hamilton Kirkyard is a monument, erected in 1828, to the four men who were captured and killed for their beliefs. John Parker, Gavin Hamilton, James Hamilton and Christopher Strang were executed at the Grassmarket, Edinburgh. The right hands of the martyrs were exhibited at Lanark, for here it was that these men had signed the Covenant. The bodies were quartered and the heads, for long, were grisly ornaments at the Old Tolbooth at Overtown.

For a few years thereafter, a more sympathetic approach by the Crown found favour and over one hundred ministers who had been "outed" or ejected returned to their parishes under two Declarations of Indulgence in 1669 and 1672. Two years later, however, in 1674, the repressive regime was once more directed against the Covenanters and the field meetings were declared to be acts of treason and, as such, punished as capital crimes.

The conventicles now became the rallying point of the Covenanting movement. The rigour of the dragoons of Charles II in suppressing the Presbyterian faith caused the Covenanters to carry arms and post pickets at the religious gatherings. Such meetings were often held in moorland areas to avoid discovery by the dragoons. The conventicles were described as great religious outpourings, made all the more intense by the strong dangers of discovery by the forces of the Crown.

The vehemence of the preaching and the resonant singing of the psalms made for scenes of great religious fervour. The 121st psalm was the favourite praise at the conventicles and its opening verse all the more poignant due to the moorland surroundings and the fear of imprisonment:

> "I to the hills will lift mine eyes
> From whence doth come mine aid.
> My safety cometh from the Lord
> Who heaven and earth had made."

Lifting your eyes to the hills and depending on the Lord for personal safety carried a most potent significance for the assembled flock.

The Covenanting fervour continued apace and in 1679 the men of Galloway rose against the brutal actions of the government army. This action came to be known as heralding the Second Resistance. To combat the zeal of the Covenanters, the Crown despatched more detachments of dragoons to attempt to pacify the uprising. These soldiers, who were labelled the "Highland Host", carried out their orders with brutality.

Archbishop Sharp of St Andrews was murdered by a group of fanatics on 3 May, 1679, and this episode was followed by a series of events which culminated in the Battle of Bothwell Brig. A public manifesto was prepared at Strathaven by a group of Covenanters, some sixty in number. They travelled to Rutherglen on Thursday, 29 May, in order to publish their testimony which came to be known as the Rutherglen Declaration. The date was purposely chosen to coincide with the unpopular statutory holiday in honour of the King's birthday and restoration. The Covenanters doused the bonfires which had been lit to celebrate the holiday and compelled the magistrates to accompany them to the market cross. The obnoxious Acts of Parliament were burned and, after prayer and praise, the Manifesto was read out and then nailed to the market cross.

Events moved rapidly now. The commander of the Royal forces, John Graham of Claverhouse, moved to the west to track down the demonstrators. He learned that a conventicle was to be held at Drumclog – a few miles west of Strathaven – on Sunday, 1 June. Claverhouse attacked the Covenanters and a pitched battle was fought. The outcome was a victory for the Covenanting forces. Claverhouse was so hotly pursued that he could not rally his men. His horse, although badly wounded by a pitchfork, carried him to safety.

The victors resolved to keep together and crowds of sympathisers flocked to them. As a result, however, of a failure to agree on a common declaration, acute dissension broke out among the Covenanters. The effect was to prevent many sympathisers from joining the cause who would otherwise have done so. The Covenanters drew up their forces on Hamilton Muir and the Hamilton declaration was posted at the Mercat Cross on Friday, 13 June, 1679. The disarray among the Covenanters caused many to defect and the lack of control in the Covenanting detachments was an ominous sign for the battle to come.

And come it did, on Sunday, 22 June, 1679, at Bothwell Brig when the Duke of Monmouth, commanding the Government forces, approached the Clyde. The Royalist forces, some fifteen thousand in number, had been reinforced with troops from the south. Although the Covenanters held the best position, their lack of discipline and control, as well as their lack of numbers, was to prove fatal. The battle lasted a mere four hours. By ten in the morning the Royal troops had gained the bridge and panic seized the Covenanting forces. More than four hundred died in the chase after the battle and one thousand two hundred were taken prison and marched to prison to Edinburgh.

> *"Along the lane, ayont the brig*
> *Mony brave men lie cauld and still*
> *But lang we'll mind, and sair we'll rue*
> *The bloody battle of Bothwell Hill."*

Several hundred prisoners were sentenced to transportation to the Americas, and many drowned when their ship sank off the Orkney Islands.

The years from 1679 to 1688 were known as "The Killing Times". The records of the Covenanters relate a number of incidents over that period involving Hamilton and District.

At Little Earnock in Hamilton, under three pine trees, were buried two brothers by the name of Smith belonging to Earnock Muir, and a man whose name has not been handed down. They had fought in the ranks of the Covenanting Army at Bothwell Brig and in the retreat had reached the upper part of the garden close to the burn where they were overtaken by Royalist soldiers and killed upon the spot.

A monument was erected to their memory but suffered much vandalism over the years. The upper section, containing a cross, was totally destroyed and steps were taken by Hamilton District Council to remove the memorial to the graveyard at Hamilton Old Parish Church where it has been erected adjacent to the memorial commemorating the deaths of the four men at Rullion Green.

On Sunday, 18 June, 1995, a Conventicle was held in the kirkyard of the Old Parish Church of Hamilton to unveil these Covenanting memorials. Pickets were posted by The Scottish Rifles and the information plaque was unveiled by the Lord Lieutenant of Lanarkshire, Hutchison R Sneddon, Esq. The proceedings were brought to a conclusion by the parish minister, The Very Reverend Dr Hugh R Wyllie, who delivered a moving address.

In the churchyard at Stonehouse lies a memorial stone to James Thomson who was shot at Drumclog for his adherence to the Word

The Covenanters' Monument, Bothwell Bridge

of God. His descendants erected this stone in 1832 which, in turn, replaced an older monument about which no information is available.

After Bothwell Brig, a Hamilton youth, Arthur Tackett, was taken to Edinburgh, questioned and tortured. He was hanged thereafter because he would not reveal when he had gone to hear the preacher, James Renwick.

In the graveyard at Dalserf Parish Church is an obelisk to the Reverend John McMillan who opposed the interference of the state in the Church and protested at the invasion of the civil magistrates upon the Church's right to regulate its meetings and manage its own affairs under the Headship of Christ.

In the same graveyard at Dalserf lies a monument to a Covenanter, Robert Laurie, who lived at Park of Mauldslie. Little more is known other than what is recorded on the stone.

At least twenty four martyrs are recorded from this area, and one hundred and forty six individuals were fined, imprisoned or outlawed.

In the year 1903 an imposing monument was erected at Bothwell Brig. The inscriptions on the obelisk read:

For Christ's Crown and Covenant
In memory
of
the Covenanters
who fought and fell in the
Battle of Bothwell Brig
22 June 1679
in defence of
Civil and Religious Liberty

Erected by public subscription
1903
The righteous shall be in everlasting remembrance
Psalm 112 : 6

Blessed are they that are persecuted for righteousness' sake
for their's is the Kingdom of Heaven
Matthew 5 : 10

Be thou faithful unto death and I will give
thee a crown of life
Revelations 2 : 10

Charles II died in February, 1685 and was succeeded by his brother as James II and VII. The struggle between the English Parliament and the Crown continued apace. The new King was adjudged to have favoured Roman Catholics and Episcopalians. Presbyterians united to withstand the Stuart claim to the Divine Right of Kings. Finally James fled to France in December, 1688, and, his daughter Mary and son-in-law, William, became joint monarchs of England in February, 1689, and two months later were proclaimed as King and Queen of Scotland by the Convention of Estates.

In May, 1689, the Cameronian Regiment (26th Regiment of Foot) was created at Douglas Dale. The regiment takes its name from Richard Cameron who became one of the most fervent Covenanters. In 1680, he declared war against Charles II. His rebellion was shortlived and he was killed in a skirmish with the Royalist forces in that same year. In 1881, the Cameronians were amalgamated with the Perthshire Light Infantry (90th Regiment of Foot), to become The Cameronians (Scottish Rifles). The combined battle honours include Blenheim, Corunna, Sebastopol, the Boer War, both World Wars, Malaya and Aden.

The Regimental Depot, which is the home of the Regiment and the training centre for new recruits, was established in Hamilton in 1881. The building was the former Cavalry Barracks and is now occupied by Bell College. In 1964, the Cameronians' Regimental HQ and Museum were transferred to Hamilton where premises were shared at Muir Street with the Burgh Museum. The Regimental Museum was opened by Lord Clydesmuir on 27 November, 1968. Since March, 1983, the Museum has been housed in the Riding School.

The Regiment was disbanded in 1968 and a special Conventicle was held at Douglas Dale on 14 May, 1968, to mark the occasion – 279 years to the day from the formation of the County Regiment.

After the end of the Covenanting Movement in 1689, memorials and martyr gravestones were erected in the West and South of Scotland. Over the intervening years many of these monuments fell into disrepair. Due to the remote nature of several of the tombs, their whereabouts disappeared from common knowledge.

In order to remedy this sad state in our Scottish history, the Scottish Covenanter Memorials Association was founded in 1966 with the object of preserving the graves and memorials of the Covenanters. The Association record, restore, repair and preserve the artefacts of the

Covenanters and in so doing provide a greater awareness of our religious and historical heritage. Local members are encouraged to have an interest in the care of the memorials in their areas. The Association is non sectarian and non political and the work of restoration is done by volunteer members and supporters who are prepared to carry out simple renovation of headstones – removing moss and soil and applying protective solutions. The more complex tasks are carried out by professional masons, the costs being met from Association funds. The members are derived from all walks of life and Hamilton and District memorials have all received restorative attention from the Association – most recently in the relocation of the Little Earnock memorial in the graveyard at the Old Parish Church of Hamilton.

Much confusion exists in the public mind about the Covenanting Movement. The general perception is of a conflict between Roman Catholic and Presbyterian. The struggle, in simple terms, was between the Episcopalian faith, the Stuart monarchy and the Divine Right of Kings against the Presbyterians who acknowledged Christ as King, opposed the introduction of bishops and the absolute right of Kings.

Of course, the issues and their protagonists are set in the standards and assumptions of those seventeenth century times. Undoubtedly there were fanatics on both sides and much brutal slaughter resulted from these conflicts. During that span of fifty years, the Scots fought fiercely for their beliefs and in so doing, suffered over eighteen thousand deaths. The Killing Times were well-named, indeed.

Hamilton and its surrounding district had a central role to play during the struggle. Bothwell Brig, the Dukes of Hamilton, Hamilton Parish Church and its preachers, the memorials to the martyrs and followers loom large in understanding the complexities of a civil war fought with bloody cruelty over three hundred years ago. We can honour today those who suffered grievously as possessing a courage matching their convictions and beliefs.

AN EXTRACT FROM "NOTES ON EDINBURGH"

"And so they were at last in their resting graves. So long as men do their duty, even if it be greatly in a misapprehension, they will be leading pattern lives, and whether or not they come to be beside a martyr's monument, we may be sure they will find a safe haven somewhere in the providence of God".

Robert Louis Stevenson

THE CAMERONIANS (SCOTTISH RIFLES)

Alison Reid

Origins

The Cameronians (Scottish Rifles) Regiment had its origin in the Covenanting period described in the chapter on Hamilton and the Covenanting Tradition.

In April 1689, the Scots Convention of Estates decided to offer the Scottish Crown to the Protestant William of Orange and his wife Mary, daughter of the Catholic James VII and II. William and Mary had been invited to take the English throne by the English Parliament, and James had fled, but Graham of Claverhouse was raising an army for him. In response, the Scottish Parliament issued a declaration to raise troops for "the service of the King's Majesty, in the defence of the nation; recovery and preservation of the Protestant Religion; and in particular, the work of Reformation in Scotland, in opposition to popery, prelacy and arbitrary power in all its branches and steps until the government of church and state be brought back to their lustre and integrity established in the best and purest terms."

Dunkeld 1689

The Earl of Angus, a young man of eighteen, responded by raising a regiment at Douglas on 14 May, 1689, "all in one day, and without beat of drum, nor expense of levy money" as it was reported at the time. In a strong Covenanting area, the men were accustomed to bearing arms and being under discipline from years of protecting field preaching meetings, called Conventicles, against government troops.

From the outset, the Regiment, known initially as Angus's after its Colonel, had a strong religious base, and held to Covenanting traditions of Protestant, Presbyterian Christianity. Until the Regiment disbanded in 1968, each recruit received a pocket bible, weapons were carried to church services and armed pickets posted. The name later adopted of Cameronians was in honour of a Covenanting Minister, Richard Cameron, killed by government dragoons at Airds Moss in 1680.

The new Regiment was in action very quickly. Claverhouse's army met and defeated government troops at Killiecrankie in July, 1689. Although Claverhouse was killed, the army moved south and Angus's regiment took part in a desperate defence of Dunkeld.

Outnumbered more than four to one, the Regiment fought for over four hours to hold off James's army, even stripping lead from the cathedral roof to make bullets. The fight was a terrible initiation for recruits. According to one eyewitness "Half the town was blazing; and with the incessant roar of the guns were mingled the piercing shrieks of wretches perishing in the flames". The village of Dunkeld was virtually destroyed by fire, but the defence held, saving Scotland from further civil war. James's forces, defeated and leaderless, disbanded. The Scottish Parliament was free to negotiate with William and Mary. The Act of Settlement saw the Presbyterian Church established by law in Scotland in 1690, and the fulfillment of one of the Covenanters' principal objectives.

The Regiment had been blooded, but had suffered casualties, perhaps the most notable being their first commanding officer, William Cleland. He had led the Covenanters at Drumclog in May 1679, against Claverhouse and government dragoons, and had also fought at the Battle of Bothwell Bridge which followed on 22 June. His memory holds a special place in the Regiment's tradition, as can be seen in the poem at the end of this chapter.

The 26th Regiment of Foot

As the threat at home receded, French expansion in Flanders took the Regiment abroad.

In their first battle at Steinkirk in 1692, the Earl of Angus was killed, but the Regiment continued to distinguish itself, first at Landen and then at Namur, until the Peace of 1697. In the War of the Spanish Succession, it served under Marlborough between 1702 and 1709 at Blenheim, Ramillies, Oudenarde and Malplaquet, in all of which it gained Battle Honours.

At Malplaquet (1709), the Regimental History records that "the Cameronians suffered severely for the cannonballs came thick among them, and swept away whole files of men." They also fought around Mons and Bethune which were to figure in the Cameronians' experiences over 200 years later in the First World War.

Campaigning was exhausting both physically and spiritually. Captain Blackader confided in his diary in May 1705 "Sabbath. Marching all day. This is what I hate most. Nothing but cursing

THE BATTLE OF TANIERES
NEAR MONTS 1709

Battle of Tanieres 1709

swearing and profaneness, as if Hell itself had broken loose about me...we have indeed a very wicked army which is a great discouragement; and I am weary of dwelling in the tents of sin."

In August 1707, he noted "the worst day for the poor soldiers I have ever seen. It poured down heavy rain, and the cavalry had so broken the way that the men marched in clay and dirt to their knees...."

The losses during the campaign called for major recruiting, much of which happened in England, so that within twenty years, there was little connection left with the original covenanting regiment. Captain Blackader sold his commission in 1711, but later raised a Volunteer Regiment in Glasgow to fight the Jacobite Rising of 1715. As a reward he was made Deputy Governor of Stirling Castle, where he remained until his death in 1727.

The Regiment also helped defeat the Jacobite rebels by storming the defences at Preston in 1715. The tune 'Kenmure's on an awa', which refers to one of the Jacobite leaders, was probably adopted at this time.

There followed a period of mixed service in garrisons, serving as crew in ships for an enlarged fleet off Spain, and defending Gibraltar against an expected assault in 1727 from Spain, who was seeking to expand her influence in the Mediterranean.

In 1751, numerical titles were given to all regiments and the Cameronians became the 26th Foot.

The Regiment was sent to America in 1767 and on to defend Canada, an impossible task with the outbreak of the American War of Independence. Scattered into small units, many of the Regiment were taken prisoner at Ticonderoga, Crown Point, and St. Johns, but were exchanged for American prisoners in British hands. They then successfully took part in attacks on Forts Clinton and Montgomery to prevent the Americans blockading the supply route up the Hudson River, before wintering in 1777 in the comparative luxury of Philadelphia, while the American army under Washington froze nearby at Valley Forge. The following year the Regiment was recalled to New York before being shipped back to England where they arrived "perfectly worn out and it will take at least two years before it can be returned fit for service" according to its new commander, Colonel Lord Adam Graham.

During the Napoleonic Wars, the 26th was sent in 1801 to Egypt where they took part in the Battle of Aboukir. They returned to Britain but war breaking out again, they sailed for Germany in 1805. Two of the troopships were wrecked, one on the Dutch coast, the other on Dogger Bank with the loss of 13 officers, 474 men, and 52 women and children between them. This was almost half the Regiment. They then returned in calmer seas to England without firing a shot in anger.

In 1808, the Regiment was sent to Spain and took part in the retreat to Corunna. An eyewitness described "Our army winding its way along the serpentine road, and the motionless blotches of red, left and right, upon the white snow indicating the bodies of those whom hunger and cold had accounted for... the dark almost polar night fell early and concealed these dreadful sights from our eyes." The 26th, with other units, beat off a French attack on their positions, enabling a successful withdrawal by sea.

The 26th was then sent to Walcheren at the mouth of the Scheldt near Antwerp, but withdrew depleted by the Walcheren fever, a malarial fever worsened by accompanying dysentery and typhus. The Regiment returned to Portugal under Wellington but was so affected by the disease that it was removed from the field and took no further part in the war.

In 1840, the 26th were sent from India to take part in the China War, and occupied the island of Chusan which led to the capture of Canton, and threatening the Chinese second city and the heart of her commercial empire, Nanking.

There followed a period of peacetime service at home and around the Empire. In 1868, it formed part of an expedition to Abyssinia (Ethiopia) to put pressure on Emperor Theodore who had imprisoned the British Consular Agent and other Europeans.

In 1881, the British Army was re-organised under the Cardwell reforms, and the 26th Foot Cameronians were linked with the 90th Perthshire Light Infantry to become the Cameronians (Scottish Rifles). The Cameronians formed the 1st Battalion of the new Regiment. As a Rifle Regiment, the soldiers worked in small groups, wearing green uniforms to help camouflage them, and maintain the element of surprise. Unlike other foot regiments they did not carry colours to advertise their presence, and the colours were 'laid up'. One set was presented to Glasgow Cathedral, the second is held in the Museum.

The Cameronians adopted tartan in 1881 along with the other Lowland regiments using the Government or Black Watch tartan. Douglas tartan was not authorised until 1891.

The Regimental badge celebrates the origins of both parties with the five pointed mullet (spur rowel) of the Douglas family to which the Earl of Angus belonged, and the Light Infantry bugle and cord of the 90th Perthshire Light Infantry.

The 90th Perthshire Light Infantry

The 90th Perthshire Volunteers were raised by Thomas Graham of Balgowan in response to a later government call for troops, this time to fight the French. Graham had a personal reason to dislike the French. His wife, Mary, had suffered from poor health. They travelled in search of a better climate, but she died in June, 1792. On the journey home, Graham related how French Revolutionary Guards "an unruly mob of half drunk rascals" had broken open his wife's coffin "with brutal violence" at Toulouse, on suspicion of finding contraband.

The Regiment had its first inspection on 13th May, 1794, and became popularly known as Graham's Greybreeks due to their uniform. Their first battle honours were won at Mandora in Egypt, in 1801, for standing firm in the face of an attack by French cavalry. One soldier remembered how "The cavalry advanced upon them with their swords raised; the 90th stood firm until the cavalry were so near the right of their line that they were going to strike at them with their swords; they then began to fire, and it ran from right to left like a rattling peal of thunder."

In 1805 the Regiment transferred to the West Indies and took part in the capture of Martinique and Guadeloupe. In 1815, they returned to Europe to form part of the Army of Occupation in Paris. The following year, the 90th was made a full Light Infantry Regiment of the permanent army, upgraded from Volunteer status.

The next major war service was in the Crimea in 1854. There, although not taking part in any major battles other than the assault on the Redan during the siege of Sebastopol, they suffered atrocious conditions of cold, poor food, clothing and disease for nearly two years. "I don't know what our Brigade Major knows but he certainly did not evince any intimate acquaintance with the duties of his office" wrote a young subaltern, Garnet Wolseley, who went on to become one of the three Commanders in Chief of the Army provided by the Regiment. Private J. Alexander won the Regiment's first Victoria Cross for rescuing a wounded officer from the Coldstream Guards who was lying exposed to enemy fire.

In 1857, the Regiment was diverted to India to assist in quashing the Indian Mutiny. One of the two ships carrying three companies, "The Transit", was hit by a cyclone off Singapore and wrecked, but without loss of life, thanks to good discipline. This delayed their arrival at Lucknow where the rest of the Regiment were involved in the Relief of the Residency, but not the town. The delayed companies later formed part of the main Relief Force, so that the 90th became the only regiment to be represented in both the besieged and relieving forces. Garnet Wolseley recalled that "Suddenly there was an explosion and out of the dust and smoke that arose from it there ran forward an officer and a number of British soldiers...To the astonishment of us all it was Captain Tinling with his company behind him. We had both too much to do to squander time in commonplace talk, but to all ranks of our two companies the meeting was indeed a hearty one."

The Regiment stayed in India for twelve years and, in 1878, were sent to South Africa to take part in the Zulu War. The 90th defeated a massive Zulu army at Kambula Hill by concentrated accurate fire, and remained on active service until the war was won at Ulundi the following year, when they returned to India.

In 1881, the 90th became the 2nd Battalion the Cameronians (Scottish Rifles). The colours were laid up in St. Mary's Church, Hamilton, and St. Giles Cathedral, Edinburgh.

The 2nd Battalion took part in the 2nd Boer War of 1899 to 1902, fighting at Spion Kop, Pieter's Hill and Vaal Krantz as part of the force sent to relieve British troops besieged at Ladysmith.

Volunteers

Men from the Cameronians' four volunteer battalions served with the regular battalions in South Africa. They came from the 1st-4th Lanarkshire Volunteer Rifle Corps, which were formed in 1859-60, each with defined recruiting areas and company depots.

The 2nd Lanarkshire Rifle Volunteers, for example, was made up of companies from Hamilton, Uddingston, Blantyre, Bothwell, Wishaw, Motherwell, East Kilbride, Strathaven and Larkhall. The headquarters were in Hamilton, close to the Depot Barracks. Its central rifle range was at Cadzow.

The Regimental Depot, which was the home of the Regiment and the training centre for new recruits, was established in Hamilton in 1881 in the former Cavalry Barracks on Almada Street.

At the 1881 reforms, the Lanarkshire Rifle Volunteers became the Cameronians' five volunteer battalions. In 1908, with Army reorganisation, the 1st, 2nd, 3rd and 4th Volunteer Battalions became the 5th, 6th, 7th and 8th Battalions the Cameronians (Scottish Rifles) of the Territorial Force.

The First World War

At the start of the War, the Regiment consisted of two regular Battalions, two Reserve Battalions and four part time volunteer (Territorial) Battalions. During the War, a further nineteen Battalions were raised to serve on the Home Front and Overseas. The 1st, 2nd, 5th, 6th, 9th and 10th Battalions served on the Western Front. The 7th and 8th served at Gallipoli, Egypt, Sinai, and Palestine and then on the Western Front, while the 11th saw service in Greece.

The 1st Battalion formed part of the British Expeditionary Force, landing in France on 15th August, 1914. It fought on the Mons-Conde Canal, at Le Cateau, on the retreat to the river Marne, the advance to the river Aisne, and at Armentieres – the first battle of Ypres.

At Neuve Chapelle, on 10th March, 1915, the 2nd Battalion went into action with 900 men. Only 152 were left to be withdrawn from the battle by March 14th. The 6th Battalion suffered a similar fate at Festubert in June, and the 7th and 8th Battalions likewise around Gully Ravine in the Gallipoli Campaign. One eyewitness recorded "it looked like a midden and smelled like an open cemetery." By July, the remnants of the two battalions were merged, and by the withdrawal in early 1916, 43 officers and 864 men had been lost.

In October, the 1st Battalion was in the thick of the fighting at Loos, and from July to October, 1916, was in the battle of the Somme. The 1st, 2nd, 5/6th, 9th and 10th Battalions were all involved, and again battle casualties accounted for the loss of half of their fighting strength. The following year, there was an advance on the Hindenburg Line at Croisilles, and the 3rd battle of Ypres, "the most severe test to which the regiment has been subjected", according to the Regimental Historian, Professor S.H.F. Johnston.

1918 involved holding out against the German 'Big Push' of the Spring, around Meteran and Strazeele. When the Allies finally advanced the 1st Battalion fought on virtually until Armistice on November 11th.

The Regiment had raised some 150,000 men, and lost over 7,100, with at least 25,000 wounded, many of whom were crippled for life.

This represented over 20% of those who had joined the Regiment. Even so this does not take into account the many local men who served in other regiments such as the Highland Light Infantry which recruited heavily from the Glasgow area.

The nineteen War Battalions and the two Reserve Battalions were disbanded. The Territorial Battalions returned to their normal peace-time role, with the 6th Battalion based in Hamilton. The 5th and 8th were joined in 1920 as the 5th/8th Battalion and in 1938 became a Searchlight Regiment Royal Artillery. In 1940, the Regimental Depot moved from Hamilton to Lanark.

The Second World War
Although the Second World War began similarly with the 2nd Battalion forming part of the British Expeditionary Force to France in September, 1939, the Regiment was to fight in all the theatres of war. After heavy losses, the 2nd Battalion was evacuated from Dunkirk, while the 6th and 7th fought around Cherbourg.

The 2nd battalion was sent to India in 1942, arriving in May, and in August pushed west into Persia and on to Damascus in 1943.

This was followed by redeployment to the invasion of Sicily as part of the Eighth Army, and the Battalion went ashore near Syracuse on 10th July, 1943. This success led to the invasion of Italy, landing near Riggio on 3rd September, and a hop on to Anzio Beachhead in March, 1944, fighting north to Rome. The Battalion was then transferred to the invasion/ N W Europe campaign where it joined the 6th, 7th and 9th Battalions till the end of the War.

The 9th landed at Arromanches in Normandy on 17th June, and suffered far heavier casualties than any other Cameronian Battalion as they were involved in almost continual fighting from then until the German capitulation. The 6th and 7th took part in the Liberation of Holland, landing at Walcheren Island, scene of previous landings by the Regiment in 1691 and 1809. This opened up the sea approaches to Antwerp, the first port facility captured by the Allies, and ensured the crucial supplies needed to support the Allied advance.

The 1st Battalion was in India at the outbreak of war, and in February, 1942 moved to Rangoon in Burma to oppose the advancing Japanese. Most of the fighting was fragmented by the jungle terrain, although battle was joined at Yenangyaung on the east bank of the Irrawaddy. The army withdrew into India in May, 1942, while further

Cameronians 6th Battalion at the Riding School, Hamilton c1939

plans were developed, centred on deep penetration of the jungle areas behind enemy lines by airborne troops.

The 1st battalion formed part of this new "Chindit" force and, after intensive training, returned to Burma in March, 1944. The five month campaign had three phases – March and April, communications disruption; May, holding a road block centre named 'Blackpool' near Hopin, and June and July, harassing the enemy south of Magaung – before being airlifted out again to India.

The campaign took place in conditions of appalling heat and monsoon, and the physical strain of continual patrol and living on limited rations supplied by air, caused severe hardship, worsened by jaundice, malaria, dysentery and other tropical diseases. By the final phase of the campaign, the Battalion was ordered to defensive positions, it was clearly so seriously debilitated.

In 1945, the Battalion was sent to South Malaya and Singapore, where, on 15th December, Lt. Col. Thomas CBE, DSO, took the surrender of all the Japanese forces serving in Singapore and South Malaya. A man of many parts, Lt. Col. Thomas had commanded the 1st Battalion during the withdrawal from Rangoon to India in 1942 with great skill and distinction. It was very fitting that, as commanding officer of the 1st Battalion again at that time, he should have the honour of receiving the surrender.

Post 1945

The 9th and 10th Battalions were disbanded soon after the end of the War and in 1947 the Regiment was reduced due to a general scaling down in the size of the army. All two battalion regiments were reduced to one, and the 1st Battalion, still stationed in India, was suspended. In August 1948, when it became clear that the suspension would be permanent, the 2nd Battalion was renamed the 1st Battalion. Two years later a similar amalgamation of Territorial Battalions merged the 6th and 7th Battalions into one.

The Regiment continued to serve around the world, with a particularly tough tour of duty in Malaya between 1950-53, and it then moved to the Rhine, before briefly returning home to Scotland. In 1958, it was on the move again to Kenya, Aden and Jordan, and was moving regularly till 1967, when it took up base at Redford Barracks, Edinburgh.

The Regiment received the Freedom of the Burgh of Lanark in

1947, after the Regimental Depot moved to Winston Barracks in Lanark. However, a further army reorganisation led to the establishment of a Regimental Headquarters back in Hamilton in 1967, in the Burgh Museum building in Muir Street. The Regimental Museum was opened by Lord Clydesmuir on 27 November, 1968. The Freedom of the Burgh of Hamilton was granted on 10 May, 1975, and received by the Territorial Battalion on the Regiment's behalf.

The years 1967-68 proved to be momentous in many ways. At that time further reductions in the army were being planned, and the decision was taken by the Regiment that it was preferable to disband than to be merged. It was believed that as Scotland's only Rifle Regiment, with a significant history in Scottish, British and world affairs, and a style reflecting the particular traditions of its two Battalions, this record and tradition would inevitably be affected by such a merger. Such a dilution was felt to be unacceptable.

Accordingly, on 14 May, 1968, the Cameronians (Scottish Rifles) Regiment was disbanded in a ceremony at Douglas, exactly 279 years after it had been raised.

The same year, the Territorial Army was disbanded, and a new Territorial and Army Volunteer Reserve established. The "52nd Lowland Volunteers" comprised companies retaining local identities, and two companies kept the Cameronian name and uniform. One company was based at Cameronian House, Hamilton, the other at Scottish Rifles House in Motherwell. In 1995, the two Battalions of the Lowland Volunteers were formed into different units again, the 1st Battalion becoming part of the 3rd (Volunteer) Battalion The Royal Highland Fusiliers, the 2nd Battalion becoming the Lowland Volunteers.

The Army Cadet Force, formed in 1942, and the Combined Cadet Force continued to provide recruits who went on to join the Regiment, and now still join the Regular Army. Since the disbandment, the Kings Own Scottish Borderers have recruited from this area.

The link with this area remains through the memories of local people who served, or had relatives serve, in the Regiment, and in the collections and archives transferred by the Regimental Trustees along with the Museum to the care of Hamilton District Council and its successor, South Lanarkshire, in 1995. These are accessible on display and by enquiry at the Museum at Muir Street, Hamilton.

AN ACROSTIK UPON HIS NAME

W ell, all must stoop to death, none dare gainsay.
I f it command, of force we must obey:
L ife, Honour, Riches, Glory of our State
L yes at the disposing Will of Fate:
I ft were not so, why then by sad loud thunder
A nd sulph'rous crashes, which rends the skies asunder
M ust a brave Cleland by a sad destiny,

C ulled out a Victime for his country die.
L o, here's a divine hand, we find in all,
E ternal Wisdom has decreed his fall.
L et all lament it, while loud fame reports,
A nd sounds his praise in Country, Cities, Courts.
N o old forgetful Age shall end his story,
D eath cuts his days but could not stain his Glory.

Written to the first Commanding Officer by an unknown Author, 1698, and included in a collection of Lieutenant-Colonel Cleland's poetry.

LARKHALL

Helen Sykes and John Milligan

Introduction

The parish of Dalserf covers an area of approximately eleven square miles, and includes the town of Larkhall and smaller settlements of Dalserf, Millheugh, Ashgill and Netherburn. It lies on the west bank of the River Clyde which forms the east and northeast boundaries of the parish. To the west and southwest lie the River Avon and the Cander Water. The parish was originally known as Machanshire, possibly from the Gaelic "Maghan", a little plain, and the Saxon "Scir" or "Shire", a division, or from the name of St Machan. The lands were owned by the ancient church of Cadihou or Cadzow. The name changed to Dalserf in the seventeenth century when the parish church was transferred from the district of Machan to a site on the banks of the Clyde. The name may originate from St Serf, "dal" being derived from the Gaelic, "dail", meaning "field" or "meadow".

Pre-Historic Settlements

The first known inhabitants of Larkhall were the Beaker People of the middle Bronze Age (1700-1300 BC). Patrickholm sand quarry, on the banks of the Avon, became famous overnight in 1947 when a workman's tools dislodged sandstone slabs, revealing a short cist containing human remains, food vessels, combs, pebble necklaces and beakers. These early people settled the lands of Lesmahagow, Stonehouse and Dalserf parishes and evidence of their later fortifications is to be found in the most southerly point of Dalserf parish, at Cairncockle.

The Romans

Between 80 and 100 AD the Romans began their invasion of modern day Scotland. They advanced following the main rivers such as the Tweed, the Nith and, in this area, the Clyde. Lollius Urbicus sent a conquering army against the local Damnonii tribes, and in 142 AD began the construction of the Antonine Wall between the Clyde and the Forth Estuaries. Expeditionary forces were sent in all directions. It is known that an army set up camp in present day Strathclyde Park, having followed the Clyde by way of Dalserf and Ross at Hamilton.

Although, however, the Venerable Bede credited the Romans with having introduced fruit growing into the Clyde Valley, when they did leave the area, any influence on the local tribes, in the way of advancement of agriculture or even a monetary system, was soon forgotten and the Damnonii went back to their primitive ways. It was left to the monks of Lesmahagow to reintroduce formal fruit growing in the thirteenth century.

The Coming of Christianity

We have seen how St Serf may have given his name to the parish of Dalserf. He was an early saint associated with a number of Scottish places, including Culross in Fife, but he is also known to have worked in the Clyde Valley during the sixth century AD. The site of the old kirk at Dalserf is thought to be the original location of St Serf's earliest church. According to legend, St Serf ordained St Mungo (or Kentigern as he was also known) at Culross and through him a long line of missionaries was created. The south of Scotland has been called the country's "Cradle of Christianity". It was here that St Ninian and his disciples first preached, here that St Kentigern founded his churches and here that St Patrick was born. The connection of the latter with the area remains in the name of Patrickholm near the Avon, and Dalpatrick ("The Field of Patrick") in the southeast of the parish, where, from the twelfth century onwards, the chapel was probably the most important religious building in the area. It later became the Chapel of St Mary, and was destroyed during the Reformation.

The other saint associated with the parish of Dalserf is St Machan. Trained in Ireland in the sixth century by Cadoc, Machan continued his work in the Clyde Valley, setting up what was possibly his main centre at Dalserf. His name is commemorated in place names round the parish – Machanhill, St Machan's Parish Church and Machan Road.

The present parish church of Dalserf was built in 1655 when the church transferred from the old chapel building at Dalpatrick. One of its best known ministers, the Reverend William Peebles Rorison, affectionately nicknamed it "The Auld Grey Mother Kirk". Though now "T" shaped, the building was originally rectangular. Seven doors exist in the church, a reminder that it was built during the Reformation, a turbulent time in Scotland's history, when the need for a hasty departure often arose! Below one of the west windows lies a reminder of the ancient occupation of the area, an slab of freestone, its sides

129

carved with four rows of scalloping, which was unearthed by the grave digger on the south side of the church in 1897. This 'hog back' monument probably belongs to the Anglian Period around 900 to 1000 AD.

The Hamiltons of Larkhall

Little is known of the early secular history of Larkhall and its surroundings. In very early times, the area probably belonged to the Crown and formed part of the hunting ground of Cadzow. For a time, during the thirteenth century, the lands were annexed by the powerful Comyn family, later reverting to Crown lands during the reign of John Balliol (1292-1296). After the coronation of Robert the Bruce, he granted the lands of Machan and Cadzow, in 1312, to one Walter fitzGilbert whose family originated from Northumberland. It is from him that the Dukes of Hamilton are descended.

The original grant of lands became divided between the descendants of Walter fitzGilbert, giving rise to three branches of the Hamilton family owning most of Dalserf parish, and playing an important part in the making of Scottish history. The three families (or septs) were the Henderson Hamiltons, whose estate took in a great part of the Clyde Valley including Dalserf Village; the Raploch Hamiltons, whose estate and mansion stood on the site of the present St Mary's RC Chapel in Larkhall, and the Broomhill Hamiltons, whose estate and family seat, the Castle of Auld Machan, overlooked the magnificent Avon Gorge. The families deliberately retained the Hamilton name, whether the connection was by blood or through marriage, in order to take advantage of the protection offered by the powerful name. Unfortunately for the local people, the high profile in national events maintained by their landed gentry resulted in the failure of the area to develop until late into the eighteenth century.

The Hamilton family were staunch supporters of the monarchy and of Roman Catholicism. In 1563, during the Reformation, a mob was on its way to the Castle of Auld Machan bent on destroying Chapel Rone, the family's private place of worship. Lady Elizabeth, wife of Sir John Hamilton, courageously went out to meet the mob and pleaded with them, promising "If ye dinnae burn it doon, I'll mak a guid barn o' it!" This duly happened and the building stood until 1724 when it fell into disrepair. The site of the former chapel lies at the present day Broomhill Avenue, just beyond the railway bridge.

The Hamilton families in the area suffered greatly because of their involvement with the ill-fated Mary Queen of Scots. Sir John Hamilton of Broomhill died of his wounds after Mary's final defeat at the Battle of Langside in 1568, his son Claud fleeing to France. On the orders of the Regent, James Stuart, an example was to be made of her supporters and Sir William Drury, Governor of Berwick, razed many Hamilton houses to the ground, including the Castle of Auld Machan. Claud returned three years later and Broomhill House was built on the foundations of the old castle.

The Hamilton family again threw in their lot with the monarchy during the troubles that led ultimately to the execution of Charles I. Claud Broomhill Hamilton, grandson of the founder of Broomhill House, supported the Royalists in the Civil War and, like his king, perished on the scaffold at Whitehall. The family also supported the monarchy in the Covenanters' Campaign. The story of the Covenanters is covered in depth elsewhere in this book, but one story concerning the Hamiltons and the Covenanters is related here because of its particular relevance to Larkhall traditions. One of the worst persecutors of the Covenanters was William Raploch Hamilton, nicknamed The Persecuting Raploch. He lies buried in the old kirkyard at Dalserf Church and, according to local tradition, parishioners would spit on his grave as they passed. The reason behind this deep-seated hatred was the laird's behaviour on his return from the Covenanters' defeat at Bothwell Bridge in 1679. Coming across a mortally wounded Covenanter, William raised his sword to kill the poor man. Just before the blade descended, the stalwart Covenanter is supposed to have cursed the laird, saying "Ye'll no dee in your bed and the hares will yet breed on your hearthstane!" The curse seems to have come true, because William fell to his death from his horse in 1688 and, soon after, his fine mansion crumbled. Wild hares can still be seen playing there, the memory of the curse lingering on in the name of Hareleeshill.

The Development of Larkhall

The village of Larkhall (for the community has never received town status) lies on the higher ground between the gorge of the Avon Water and the river Clyde. The name derives from "Laverockhall" meaning "Lark on the Hill", and the Anglicised "Larkhall" came into use around the mid-seventeenth century.

In the early 1700s, a cluster of "farm towns", or hamlets with a working farm at the centre, had stood on the site of the present Larkhall, with names such as Raploch, Crossgates, Lav'rock'ha, Muirshot and East and West Mauchan. The farm towns gradually merged and expanded with the selling off of plots of land in the Raploch Estate, to form the village of Larkhall. By 1791, Larkhall had overtaken Dalserf to become the largest village in the district, one reason for which being the refusal by the landowners, the Henderson Hamiltons, to grant leases for any longer period than one year. By contrast, since around 1774, ninety nine year leases of land were being granted at Larkhall. The economy of the area also began to improve as a result of the Act of Union in 1707 which encouraged free trade between Scotland and England, and the agricultural revolution of the eighteenth century improved the yield from the land. As Dalserf's population dwindled, Larkhall grew in size, by 1831 having 139 houses and a population of 963, compared with 19 houses and 111 inhabitants in Dalserf.

Another reason for the development of Larkhall was its location on the intersection on the main London/Carlisle/Glasgow coach road, the Glasgow/Lanark road and the Edinburgh/Ayr road which crossed the Clyde at Garrion Bridge. Until recently a heavy iron ring was embedded in the stone wall at the corner of London Street and Wellgate Street, a reminder of bygone days when a horse changing station stood on the site. By 1840, there was a daily stage coach from Edinburgh to Ayr, another between Strathaven, Stonehouse and Glasgow, and a third between Glasgow and Lanark. The London Mail also passed through the parish at stated hours on its way to and from Glasgow. Since the present government introduced bus privatisation, it has become practically impossible to get in and out of Larkhall after 7.00 pm. Perhaps they should bring the stage coach back!

The third main factor in Larkhall's growth was the boom in the handloom weaving industry. Technological development in the form of the "spinning jenny" had made it possible to spin large quantities of cotton yarn in mills at places like New Lanark and Blantyre. Weaving this yarn into cloth was another matter and up until the early nineteenth century, it could only be done on large hand operated looms. The basic skill of weaving was relatively simple to learn and Glasgow cotton manufacturers like James Buchanan and David Dale recruited whole families to work handlooms in their own homes. In the early days of the growth of the industry, weaving was a lucrative occupation, and many people were attracted to Larkhall, often buying houses with

The Bleachfields, Millheugh

Larkhall Cross and Wellgate Street

custom-built workrooms to carry the looms. The numbers of men searching for work swelled at the end of the Napoleonic wars in 1815 when the disbanded soldiers came home. The Larkhall and Pleasance Building Society had opened in 1814, building houses on the lands of Auld Machan (West Machan). The row of houses called the Pleasance was completed in 1816. It was followed by the Larkhall Building Society in 1824. Once all its members had been provided with houses, the Building Society would be dissolved. The houses were often built to a pattern. One window looking out onto the street would be much larger than any of the others in order to catch as much daylight as possible for the operator working the "pirns" or bobbins. This feature was more apparent in some of the older houses when weaving was still a reasonably profitable business. This has resulted in Larkhall's characteristic style of housing facing directly onto the street with front gardens often absent. There were eventually so many home-owners among the working people of Larkhall that at one time the town became known as the "town of bonnet lairds". Many of the streets in Larkhall still have rows of weavers' cottages and, until recently, the Avon Bank bleachworks stood at Millheugh. Unfortunately, the employment market became overprovided, prices fell and the industry went into decline. The introduction of power looms and factory weaving in the 1840s proved to be the death knell of handloom weaving.

A legacy of the area's connections with the cloth manufacturing trade still exists in the presence of the Daks Simpson factory. This company originally came from Perrivale in London and took over Miller Street's ailing silk factory which had been in operation since 1879 when Messrs Young Caldwell and Company had employed a large number of Larkhall women. Foreign competition, especially from the Indian subcontinent, had eaten into the business after the First World War and the looms had lain virtually silent by the time the German Luftwaffe persuaded Daks that Lanarkshire was a little safer. Now it is Larkhall's biggest employer with a workforce of around 1,700 people.

As the weaving industry went into decline, another of Larkhall's natural assets came to the fore. Early coal workings date back to the mid 1400s in the Avon Gorge, but the documented earliest coal workings in and around Larkhall date from circa 1760. These were at Raploch, Skellyton, Nityard and Marlage.

Papers, belonging to the 7th Duke of Hamilton, report on the coal grieve (clerk) fiddling the books at Skellyton Colliery in 1766. He had been given what in modern day terminology would be a verbal warning by the Duke's mine overseer, John Burrel!

It was, however, with the coming of the railways in 1854, that the coal industry really took off when the Coatbridge iron masters, the Duke of Hamilton and others financed the Lesmahagow Guarantee Railway Company. Taken over four years later by the Caledonian Railway Company, the railway expanded and new coal pits sprung up all the way to Lesmahagow and Douglas. The Mid Lanark Branches, opened in 1905 through Larkhall Central, were part of this process. The period 1860-1930 witnessed the rapid growth, and equally spectacular collapse, of the coal industry in Larkhall and its surrounding districts. Now even the remains of abandoned railway tracks and coal bings (spoil heaps) are disappearing.

It was during this time that one of Larkhall's heroes emerged. Robert Smillie, local miner and trade union official, became the President of the Miners' Federation of Great Britain and Labour MP for Morpeth, Northumberland. But it was as President of the Miners that he is principally remembered, fighting for improved pay, conditions, decent housing and assistance for miners' families whose main breadwinner was unable to work any longer through pneumoconiosis, or Miner's Lung, and other conditions.

Another legacy of the collieries is the larger than average number of church buildings of all denominations. Protestants from Ulster and Roman Catholics from Southern Ireland came looking for work in nineteenth century Scotland and settled in the industrial towns of Northern Lanarkshire, bringing their own religious practices with them.

The last and perhaps the most important factor in the development of Larkhall is the people themselves. The writer of the New Statistical Account wrote disapprovingly of the manufacturing classes of Larkhall who were "too often very pestiferously busy in regard to politics and church and state affairs – trying to reform the institutions of the country, instead of trying to reform themselves". These traits however, showed themselves in very positive terms in all the self-help schemes which the workers in the area devised to improve their standard of living. We have already seen the development of the building societies which enabled people to buy their own home and work place, and Larkhall also had several friendly societies into which the workers would pay a weekly sum to safeguard against sickness.

Larkhall was one of the first villages in Scotland to have its own co-operative movement, which first appeared as the Victualling Society in premises on Hamilton Street in 1821, moving to Wellgate Street in 1830 and ultimately locating in Union Street in 1894. A second Co-op opened in Montgomery Street in 1879, based on temperance principles, but the two societies existed side by side. The concept behind the movement was to provide reasonable prices not only for food, but clothing, footwear, medicine and even an early form of health insurance, to ordinary working people, and to pay out to its customers a dividend. In the early days of the movement, the dividend was collected by customers in the form of wooden checks, oval for the Victualling Society and round for the Montgomery Society, and these would be traded in at the appropriate Co-op's. Later on, customers would receive a Co-op number, to be quoted on every purchase, and credited against their dividend. In 1969, the Scottish Co-operative Wholesale Society took over the Montgomery Street Co-op and the Victualling Society followed in 1970.

Sport and Leisure

Larkhall and its surrounding villages have a proud tradition on the sporting front with the Dicksons, Smiths, McStays, Telfers and the Crosses of Netherburn playing for sides such as Kilmarnock, Rangers, Celtic, Hibernian, Dundee United and Newcastle United. Some started with the local junior team such as Larkhall Thistle (founded 1878) and the Royal Albert which takes its name only from the old senior side, Royal Albert Athletics. The other junior side, Larkhall United, who played at Bryce's Field, folded in 1921. Their park became the venue of Larkie Fair for many years, and houses now occupy the site.

The other sports that are synonymous with the area are a cycle club (The Royal Albert Cycle Club), bowling, golf and quoits at Birkenshaw where the Falconer family has dominated at world level for generations.

Surrounding Larkhall

A number of smaller communities lie adjacent to Larkhall, each with its own history. Eighteenth century Dalserf had a thriving population of over 1,000, with six inns and a ferry across the Clyde, sited at the Boathouse near the church. We have already seen how

Dalserf declined as Larkhall expanded, and it is now a quiet village of old cottages and a picturesque church.

Rosebank lies further down the Clyde Valley, a Victorian village built by the first Lord Newlands of Mauldslie for his estate workers.

Netherburn and Ashgill were built to house the miners working in the neighbouring pits. The pits are now closed and most of the workers commute to Hamilton and nearby towns. Swinhill, Shawsburn and Cornsilloch were all once miners' rows.

Millheugh lies on the banks of the River Avon and was once a separate village, with its own brewery, distillery, waukmill (wauking was a process where the cloth was shrunk and beaten to give it a felted texture) and inkle factory (inkle was a coarse tape or material). It grew up at this location because it was the safest point to cross the river, and a ferry operated from its banks. The Applebank Inn still stands in Millheugh and was recorded as far back as 1714 when it was described as "The Applebank Alehouse, Millheugh . . . Proprietress: Big Lizzie"!

Larkhall: The Present

Diversification of industry, both in manufacturing and in services, has been part of the key in Larkhall's regeneration since 1945. The older, staple industry of coalmining and associated brick making has gone, and that legacy of the past, the abandoned bing, has been largely cleared or landscaped, making way for a wide variety of new industries and giving the local economy a boost and a fresh impetus as we approach the millennium. Major economic objectives linked to private and public housing development have succeeded in offering a wide range of work for its 16,000 inhabitants.

Daks Simpson, the well known clothing manufacturer, employs over 1,700 people and is set to expand further. Nearby lies the new Tilling Plastics Complex, recently expanded, with one hundred additional employees, manufacturing injection moulded plastic components, with a comprehensive in-house manufacturing unit, including assembly, spray painting, ultra sonic welding and printing facilities. Apprentices taken on are given training towards their HND Certificates. Investment in the introduction of robots into that factory in the moulding shop and painting section ensures a long term commitment to Larkhall. Other major employers are Hunter Douglas, the local authority, CWS Limited and Verichrome Plating Services. Plans are under consideration to link the M74 motorway skirting the town with the M8, and the proposed M74 extension towards Glasgow Airport can only assist future development. Plans to re-open the rail link to Hamilton and Glasgow are also under consideration. With further expansion in housing and services on a large scale both in Larkhall and on its northern boundary towards Hamilton, there is a newfound, well-placed optimism in the future for Larkhall's inhabitants.

LARKHA' BONNIE LASSES

An extract.

While Nature, wi' her fairy wand,
Is hills and glens adorning, O;
And lav'rocks, wi' their choral sang,
Awake the summer's morning, O -
Come, gentle muse, inspire my theme,
While I ascend Parnassus, O,
That I may, wi' poetic flame,
Sing Larkha's bonnie lasses, O.

I've seen the farmer's rosy maid
Sae lichtly trip the gowan, O,
And I've seen those in bower and glade
Wi' youth and beauty glowing, O;
I've seen them dressed at fashion's ca',
Amang the sillered classes, O;
But humble robes and virtues a'
Adorn the Larkha' lasses, O.

Gae climb the bonnie heather hills,
Or roam the flow'ry valleys, O,
And scan the maids whose beauty fills,
With pride the cot and palace, O;
Diana may at each have thrown,
A garland as she passes, O;
But Beauty sits on Virtue's throne,
And smiles on Larkha' lasses, O.

Then gather roun, ye faithfu' joes,
While youthful beauty passes, O,
To cheer you through this waste of woes
With smiles and fond caresses, O.
And while the hill of life you tread,
As time it onward passes, O,
You'll bliss the day that you were wed
To Larkha' bonnie lasses, O!

Andrew Fisher, Poems and Songs (c. 1890)

THE STORY OF THE TEXTILE INDUSTRY IN HAMILTON DISTRICT

Terry F Mackenzie

"The labouring classes in Hamilton consist chiefly of handloom weavers and workers of lace" - *Rev. William Buchan*

In 1838, when the Reverend Buchan of St John's, Hamilton, made these comments, there was a serious challenge to the district's role as an important centre of textiles in Scotland. The position was so grave that a Government Commission had been appointed to investigate the large scale depression in the trade throughout Britain.

The Hamilton area has been involved in textiles from early times to the present day, and the industry has played a greater or lesser part in local life at different periods.

Hamilton District was both typical of the trade throughout Britain and also an important player in the Scottish arena. Prior to the industrial revolution and the use of cotton in the late eighteenth century, the textile trade was in linen and wool. Apart from Hamilton bobbin lace and a wool factory, both set up through aristocratic intervention, the Hamilton area was similar to most other textile regions in Scotland.

Hamilton Wool Factory

Anne, Duchess of Hamilton (1651-1716), set up a wool-weaving factory in Hamilton between 1660 and 1705. The factory gave employment to townspeople and, when it was well-established, the Duchess gifted it to the town in 1706. At this time it had a damask loom, which made fine damask or table linen, and used a very advanced technique in its manufacture. The factory was extensive with many different areas including loom shops, warehouses, garrets and a warping room. Its value amounted to over a third of the entire valuation role of the Burgh in 1706.

Handloom Weaver at Work, Stonehouse

Hamilton Bobbin Lace

Duchess Anne has often been credited with beginning the lace industry in Hamilton, but her biographer, Dr Rosalind Marshall, has found no evidence to suggest this. The Statistical Account of Scotland, compiled in the 1790s from reports supplied by the parish ministers of the Church of Scotland, gives a tantalisingly vague account of the origins of the lace industry in Hamilton. A small scale industry was already in existence when the 'Beautiful Duchess', Elizabeth Gunning (1734-90), soon after becoming Duchess of Hamilton, established a local lace making school. A contemporary writer recorded how she "in 1752 ordered a house to be set up in Hamilton for the reception of twelve poor girls and a mistress. The girls are to be taken in at seven; to be clothed and fed and taught to read and spin etc. and to be dismissed at fourteen. What they gain by their work is to be their own, and to be given them at the end of their time. The whole is to be under the inspection of four trustees."

Lace could be made using small bobbins to work the fine linen thread into an intricate pattern around pins on a 'pillow', like a large pin cushion. By wearing lace herself, the Duchess led a fashion revival of lace in Scottish society. The thread was made from locally-grown flax. The best local thread spinners were Ann Leslie and her three sisters of Whitehill House, situated between Bothwell Road and Burnbank, and now demolished. The flax they used was grown in Uddingston and won a national competition in 1763.

Fashion changes and the death of their patroness in 1790, may have been the factors which led to a rapid decline in Hamilton Lace production.

In the 1790s, the principal occupation of Hamilton women was the spinning of linen yarn, which was sent to England and, prior to a native industry being developed there, to Northern Ireland.

Local weavers also used the linen yarn, and it, too, was a cottage industry, mainly supplying the needs of the local area. Both spinners and weavers used hand-tools and hand-operated machines. The whole family, both young and old, participated in the various processes, such as winding the yarn from the spools supplied by the agents onto smaller bobbins for the handloom.

To work as a weaver or any other trade in Hamilton, people had to pay a fee to the Town Council, thus becoming a Burgess. The Town Council of Hamilton controlled the burgess scheme and in 1738 made a further condition that all Burgesses must be residents of the Burgh.

The Industrial Revolution Comes to Hamilton District

One of the most significant inventions which triggered the industrial revolution in the textile industry was the flying shuttle. Previously, weavers could only work cloth to the maximum width of their spread arms, and needed one or two men to help them weave. The flying shuttle was thrown across the loom from side to side by levers operated by the weaver, thus allowing one man alone to weave. The following surge in demand from the weavers for spun yarn resulted in the spinners being unable to keep up with the demand. This in turn led to the automation of spinning and the establishment of large mills with thousands of spindles.

Water was a cheaper source of power than steam and so the mills were situated near a steady supply of water to provide the energy needed to drive the machinery.

A combination of several factors was at work in the development of Hamilton and Blantyre as centres of the new cotton trade. The two great ports of Glasgow and Liverpool were the main points of import of foreign cotton, first from India and then from North America.

Pre-existing skills in the Hamilton area made a rapid switch to cotton work possible. The damp climate of the Clyde valley was suitable for the siting of cotton mills as the fine yarn was less inclined to break when moist.

All these factors, together with the invention of large, powered spinning machines, made possible the opening by David Dale of a large-scale cotton spinning factory at Blantyre in 1785.

"A Fairy Neuk of Creation" – Blantyre Mill

The works as planned consisted of a spinning mill, dyeworks and dam. The dam was the subject of a lawsuit in 1839 by the proprietors of the fishing rights in the Clyde, who claimed that it prevented the free movement of fish up the river. Later still, the dam had to be increased in height as subsidence caused by coal-mining had reduced the fall of water, and so the power available to the mill.

In 1804, a Turkey red dyeing process was introduced, using the Turkish madder plant to supply the colour.

The mill's growth continued until the mid-nineteenth century, and the number of looms in the weaving shop rose from 463 to 600 in 1840. The cotton spinning trade was in decline by 1860, and in 1904 Henry Monteith & Co. was liquidated. In 1906, the mill was refitted to produce wood flour, which was used in the manufacture of linoleum. Many of the tenements of the mill village were in disrepair by 1913, and demolition began in 1925.

Four years after production began in 1787, the mill employed 520 operatives. The First Statistical Account listed 295 men, women and children. In the mill village, there were 56 widows and wives at home and 96 children too young to work.

In 1839, Robert Orr, who had been the cashier at Blantyre Mill for twenty three years, reported that the poor of the mill were taken care of by a committee of twelve workers. They met weekly to decide allowances, rates and duration of support, and levied workers for contributions. There was no obligation to pay, but if a worker did not contribute "he got warning to remove". Mr Orr was therefore able to claim that no one had refused to contribute in the twenty two years since the scheme was first introduced.

Entertainment for the workers included a soiree, the first of which was held in 1839. 'The Glasgow Herald' reported "The proceedings were enlivened by the gratuitous services both of the Sabbath school vocal band, and the instrumental band belonging to the works."

A medical report by Sir David Barry on the Blantyre Mill in 1833 described the mill as "charmingly situated". His comments on the mill itself are in sharp contrast: "the night soil falls into removable receptacles, which are removed every day; there is one in each working room, and the same privy is used by males and females. There are no washing, eating or dressing rooms. The spinning flats are close and hot, and there is an unpleasant smell from the privies...nor have any improvements tending to promote health been effected in this mill since the year 1786" (i.e. in nearly 50 years).

Sir David interviewed Mary Hunter aged 27, a power loom weaver for four years. Her father had died when she was an infant and she had been "at mill work since five years of age when she stood half the day. Remarkably straight, well-shaped, tall and handsome, has been at one time eight weeks off her work within one year. Works now to support her mother."

In visiting the homes of the spinners, all of whom were male, he found them well housed and everyone over six years old worked in the mill. At breakfast the children ate porridge and milk; with coffee, eggs, bread, oatcake and butter for the father.

The Parish Minister around 1840 claimed that the mill-workers were "living in one of the 'fairy neuks' of creation, religious and moral, well fed and clothed, and not overwrought, they seem peculiarly happy as they ought to be".

Around 1820, Sir John Sinclair calculated that 90% of the entire Scottish workforce was employed in the textile industry. In Hamilton alone, there were over 4,000 weavers by 1841.

The trade in this area was controlled by Glasgow merchants who imported the raw cotton, sent it to the mills to be spun into yarn, supplied the weavers with yarn and collected the finished cloth for sale.

Within the cotton trade, there were many fluctuations which concealed, for a time, the fact that, by 1850, the industry was in a general decline. There were, however, variations within the district. In Larkhall and Stonehouse, the number of handlooms operating actually increased between 1823 and 1836. Hamilton and Bothwell which had the higher proportion of looms, both began to suffer reduction in numbers. In 1851, the number of weavers in Hamilton had fallen to 1,222. These numbers were now eclipsed by the tambourers.

Hamilton Tambour Lace

The word tambour comes from the method of stretching lace netting tightly over a frame like a tambour or drum. In the early nineteenth century, it became possible to machine-produce lace netting, which in turn brought about a revival of lace production in Hamilton. An advantage of this system was that beautiful designs could be added to the plain lace net. The trade came to Hamilton by accident. In 1808, a shortage of labour in Paisley led to a consignment of net being sent to Hamilton to be worked. In the 1820s, women from the English lace-making town of Nottingham came to teach their skills in Hamilton. The lace agent system operated in a similar way to that in the weaving trade. By 1835, there were 2,500 women working tambour lace in Hamilton and, as the Parish Minister reported, "contributing greatly to the happiness and comfort of the community". Their products were exported worldwide.

"In Weaving, Strength is Better Paid Than Skill" – Overproduction

By 1820, handloom weaving had reached an all-time low. The County Council of Lanark met at Hamilton on 4 January, 1820, to consider the plight of the distressed weavers, when Lord Belhaven proposed a scheme of emigration for the unemployed. Robert Brown, Factor to the Duke of Hamilton, made an impassioned plea for Government intervention. "The sufferings of the Lanarkshire operatives have as much a national character as those of the cottagers of Ross-shire and Invernesshire and the relief of the one is as much a national duty as that of the other." Public subscriptions were raised.

Robert Brown had not been idle in urging local landowners and public bodies to make improvements to public amenities such as roads and bridges to provide work for the unemployed. His energy was recognised by those he helped. In 'The Glasgow Herald' of January, 1820, it was reported that "a considerable number of the operative weavers and others employed on the public roads near Hamilton waited on Mr Brown... and presented him with a neat silver cup, with a suitable inscription, expressive of their due sense of gratitude for the zeal displayed by that Gentleman in alleviating their sufferings in time of unparalleled distress".

Government Commissions discovered that, when the prices first began to dip, the weavers worked harder to produce more cloth, thus depressing the price still further.

Cotton's 'Black Economy'

Some contemporary commentators were convinced that part of the weavers' problems was caused through a form of black economy. Mr Symonds, an expert witness to a commission on the poor in Lanarkshire in 1839, reported "after careful investigation, I am compelled to believe that though there may be many exceptions among them, the majority of these small manufacturers purchases stolen weft." He went on to claim that "it is stolen by factory girls from the mills, from the warehouses by the persons employed in them and in a great measure by the women who wind pirns and to whom it seems too great a temptation to be resisted to dispose of a spindle of weft." It was distributed secretly by women pretending to sell crockery door to door, in a shadow system of the merchants' official travelling agents. The conspiracy was even wider, according to this well-informed reporter – "the police officers and certain superintendents of police are more than suspected of compromising these cases of theft, for money".

As to putting a stop to this serious evil, one Procurator Fiscal declared that the law relating to textiles was so complex "that it cannot be expected that...the public prosecutor and far less a private individual will interfere to check the crime of embezllement [sic]". In fact it was left to the weavers themselves, through their union, to tackle the problem.

Weavers' Unions

Trade unionism was not as successful amongst weavers as in the situation of the mill workers. The four main objects of weavers' unions were said at the time to be withdrawing the workmen from their employer's control; making the wages of each class of worker equal; raising wages or what is the same, preventing their fall and, in order to accomplish the other three aims, attempting to limit the number of workers in each trade.

The 1839 commission on the poor in Lanarkshire heard "As respects masters, the injury [by unions] is generally confined to property, though cases have occurred...more frequently in Scotland and Ireland [than in England] of masters opposed to particular combinations having been wounded, maimed or assassinated". The witness, however, cited no actual cases. Mr Symonds further claimed, of an incident in Airdrie, that "the military were in one instance, I was informed by the sheriff of Lanarkshire, employed to protect weavers whilst working during a strike in a colliery." This showed an interesting contrast where, on the one hand, the weavers were active in their unions and, on the other, they were willing to break the strike of another union.

The Scottish weavers' union was formed, collapsed and reformed several times. The single most important event in the weaving unions' history was the Scottish weavers' strike of 1812. This was an attempt by the union to introduce a fixed price for their work. A recent legal case involving paper makers had given the union leaders hope that their strike would not be outlawed. Within days of the strike being called, 40,000 looms in Scotland were idle. Union officials declared that "from the German Ocean [North Sea] to the Irish Channel no cotton weaver is working below the full price." At that time strikers and their families had no claim on the 'benefit' system administered by parishes, and despite determination and aid from sympathisers, the starving weavers went back to work after twelve weeks. Some of their leaders were imprisoned and the families of the committee members made liable for the debts of the now dissolved union. The trial itself aroused deep feelings of injustice among weavers. At the trial, when the weavers' defence lawyer rose to speak, all the lights in the court room except those on the bench were ordered to be put out. This resulted in the newspaper reporters being unable to see to write, and thus the newspapers carried a garbled and cut down version of the four hour speech.

Union activity was ended, at least at national level, for the next twelve years until the repeal of the Combination Acts which had banned union activity. Within weeks of the union being reformed it had enrolled over 13,000 members, including a branch in Hamilton. The union played a major role in cutting out theft by introducing a ticket system solely for accredited workers, ensuring they only could take part in the legal trade in cotton. It was, however, the next severe downturn of trade in 1825 which ended the union's effectiveness. Starving men could not afford the dues and a further attempt in the 1830s to form a union led to a similar result.

The reasons for this failure were identified in the commission's report at the time as "hand loom weavers are very much scattered over the country, and work individually in their own shops, instead of being congregated in factories; this renders it more difficult for them to combine".

Weavers were prominent in several political movements, which were active during times of distress. An attempt to replace the Government by force, known as the Radical Rising of 1820, was the first of these. Pearly Wilson of Strathaven, accused of leading the 'rebellion', was kept in Hamilton Tollbooth after his capture. Later he was taken to Glasgow where he stood trial and was hanged, then beheaded before a huge crowd.

The Corn Law agitation from about 1835 to 1846 to change government grain policies, which had led to high prices for bread, involved many weavers. Similarly, they took part in the movement for reform of the electoral system, many hoping that having a say in government would lead to intervention to better the lot of weavers, while others felt that their status had now earned them the vote.

"Often an Idle Day" – Weavers' Conditions

Handloom weaving was little subject to Government regulation. In the 1830s, the weavers' hours were seventy per week, exclusive of meal breaks. They worked from 5.00 am to 10.00 am Saturdays. Monday was "often an idle day", the remaining sixty five hours having to be worked Tuesday to Friday. The Government inspectors found

Girl at Loom, Hamilton Weaving Factory, Peacock Cross c1900

that a number of tasks which were not technically weaving took up "a considerable portion of the 70 hours". The opinion at the time was that conditions were better in the power loom factories, where everything was set up for the weaver, the yarn was of a higher quality and, being away from home, there were fewer temptations to idle.

Weavers and the Community
Two Hamilton weavers were made burgesses of the town by a grateful Town Council in 1743 for rescuing two baillies who, as the Town Council minutes record, were "being attacked by one of the Duke's servants".

"I could name 40 or 50 people who were hand-loom weavers who are now [1839] men of capital and character filling high positions", claimed an expert witness to a government enquiry.

Switch to silk weaving
By 1840, handloom weaving was entering its final phase in the district. Power looms and competition from other parts of Britain and overseas led to a long-term decline in handloom weaving in this area. Many of the handloom weavers were forced to seek other employment. Change happened fastest where there was an alternative source of work. In rural areas the number of looms actually increased.

At that time power looms could not weave high-quality silk. Many hand loom weavers were able to turn to making this new material. The industry grew up in Hamilton, Larkhall, Stonehouse and Glassford (as well as Strathaven). The weavers were supplied with silk yarn by local agents. The last of the weavers, Robert and James Hamilton of Stonehouse, stopped working in 1939.

Hamilton Cloth Factory
Sited at Peacock Cross and adjacent to the two Railway stations at Hamilton West, the factory opened in 1855 and, by 1863, employed 400 hands comprising 60 men and boys and 340 girls. It was the only mill in Scotland using a certain method of manufacture. One loom shop had 216 power looms, kept behind a sound-proof door because of the deafening noise. It was "one of the sights of Hamilton", boasting a revolving advertising sign which changed every three minutes for each of its ten messages. It supplied cloth "direct to the public". Later in Hamilton, factories opened for making women's pinafores, chenille,

151

carpet and tartan. Now only the tartan factory survives, making goods for Scotland's tourist industry.

The District's Textile Heritage

From early times until the present, the textile trade has been one of the most enduring industries in Hamilton District. The trade has seen many changes, particularly since 1785. For the greatest part of its long history, and at its peak, it has been a cottage industry.

Every part of the district has shared in the textile story. Bothwell actually had a greater proportion of weavers of the whole population than Hamilton. From the 1840s, the rural parts of the district became more important, particularly when the industry was in decline elsewhere. The reasons for this are at present unknown, and need further study. A fascinating story in its own right is how the building societies in Larkhall financed the erection of many distinctive weavers' cottages. These had two apartments – one for the family to live in, and the other a loom shop.

It has left its mark in Stonehouse, and particularly Larkhall, where the former weavers' cottages are an integral part of the urban landscape. At its peak, in Hamilton, Bothwell and Blantyre, the textile trade probably directly employed a greater proportion of the population than any industry before or since.

THE WEAVERS' STONE

Terry F Mackenzie

The Paisley weavers formed the first Friendly Society in Scotland in 1702. The Hamilton weavers formed a Friendly Society in 1728, to provide benefits to their members. It continued to do this until 1845. The members' contributions were topped up by the profits from the part of the Hamilton Wool factory which had been gifted to the Society by the Town Council in 1728. Both bad harvests and the Corn Laws which fixed the price of grain affected the whole community, and the Society took on wider responsibilities than those of its members. In addition to caring for their members, the Society, in partnership with other local societies, purchased grain outwith the Town, and supplied it for the townspeople affected by starvation. This occurred in the years 1740-2, 1772-3 and around 1800. The Society voted to provide money to employ Counsel in Parliament to oppose the Corn Laws in 1774. At other times, the Society was prosperous and loaned out money. They owned a tenement in the Townhead of Hamilton, where the cinema now stands. Prior to that they had part of David Marshall's property in the old High Street, on the site of the present Strathclyde Park. The weavers' stone from their offices has for many years been on display outside the Museums in Muir Street. Its inscription reads:

> *The art of weaving*
> *is renouned so*
> *that rich nor poor*
> *without it cannot go*

QUARTER AND LIMEKILNBURN

Julia Bearne

Quarter and Limekilnburn are on the eastern hill side of the Clyde Valley. Little stops the warm south westerly breezes in summer or the cold northern winds in winter. The views from the villages, on a clear day, can be breathtaking.

In the earliest records, Quarter, as people know it now, was called Darngaber. The remains of Darngaber Castle stand to the south of Quarter and the east of Crookedstone where, in 1679, Gordon of Earlston was killed by Government Dragoons, after the defeat of Covenanters at Bothwell Bridge. They then rode off to Carscallan Farm to display their trophies and on to Hamilton.

The standing stone at Crookedstone, just between the two villages, is a testament to the history of the area. The remains of early lime kilns in the burn near Limekilnburn, at Boghead Farm, show where the mining of limestone took place. A few miners' cottages stood there until the 1850s.

Lime was used as a fertiliser for the land as well as being used in the production of iron. Boys as young as thirteen years were responsible for very dangerous tasks such as "puddling" pig iron, converting it into wrought iron.

The Dukes of Hamilton utilised the richness of the mineral deposits of the area to help finance the estate from a very early time. The formation of the Clyde Valley meant that the coal seams were easily accessible without a deep pit shaft.

A pillar and stall or stoop and room system was used where the seam emerged. This meant that a chamber was carved where the seam was easily worked and when the coal seam was finished, the pillar of coal supporting the roof was removed and the chamber collapsed. The men and older boys worked at the coal face and the women and smaller children dragged the hutches of coal to the surface. The hutches were then drawn to the White Bridge at Chatelherault from where the coal was distributed.

The mine workings at Avonbank Colliery and Quarter were connected by drainage shafts. It was common for the workers to move between the pits. Coal and ironstone were mined in the same area although, because the seams tended to be narrower, the ironstone work was far more dangerous. The early miners worked a "piece rate" system, each hutch earning a fixed rate.

The Coaliers' Friendly Society was formed in Quarter in 1799 when miners were freed from virtual serfdom to the mine owners. Before that time the mine owners had almost owned the miners and their families. A contemporary writer, Archibald Cochran, had likened the miners to "Negro slaves in colour and manner". The aim of the Society was to support the miners and their families when they could not work as well as to represent the miners at meetings with the mine owners.

The early nineteenth century brought a boom in industry throughout Scotland. There had already been a certain amount of immigration from other coal mining areas of Britain, but with the increased amount of work in the United Kingdom as a whole, more men were drawn into the neighbourhood from other countries, Ireland in particular.

There had been for some time small mining communities at High Quarter, Laigh Quarter, the Divoty by Laigh Quarter and Darngaber Farm for the miners employed at Avon Braes. The larger of them was Laigh Quarter, with thirty one dwellings and approximately one hundred and sixty eight inhabitants. The Divoty had about six dwellings. South Quarter was, and still is, a farm. Darngaber Schoolhouse is all that remains in the present village of Quarter of what was standing at the time. Limekilnburn was a hamlet of eighteen houses. The houses were built from rough stone with a roof made of sods of earth or later, a thatch of sticks, and a dirt floor.

The miners were paid according to how much coal they dug. A tally marker was put on each hutch of coal sent to the surface. At the end of the shift the amount of coal was added up. This system was open to abuse by dishonest miners and checkers. In 1832 a miner could hope to earn 1/6d (1½p) for each ton of coal.

In 1854, the discovery of a rich seam of ironstone by Quarter led to Colin Dunlop and Company being leased the mineral working by the Dukes of Hamilton. This was a father and son company who were ironmasters of Tollcross in Glasgow. They made an enormous impact on the area.

With the arrival of Colin Dunlop's company in the area, and the building of two blast furnaces in 1857, the population of the villages rose from about 299 people to 853 in 1861. With the building of "miners' rows" for the workers at the ironworks on the edge of the village, Darngaber became a village. The ironworks were built on the road out of the village towards Hamilton, where a crossroad already existed. The mine offices were built there a few years later.

The village at Laigh Quarter grew too, as the number of ironstone miners employed at the ironworks grew. The main ironstone pit was just between Laigh Quarter and the ironworks, so the first of many railway lines was built to ship the iron ore to the furnaces.

The houses built for the workers were typical of the day, a "but and ben" or a "single end". A "but and ben" is a two roomed house, a "single end", a one roomed house on the end of the row. All of these had an outside toilet and water pump, shared by about twelve families. It was not uncommon for a family to number seven or eight, all living in one small house.

The wives tried to help the family budget by working from their homes making bobbin lace, introduced by the Duchess of Hamilton, or by selling the white clay found all around the area to the households of Hamilton to whiten the front doorstep, or for making clay pipes. The clay was also used in the Tile Works by Darngaber, a thriving business which traded until the turn of the century.

The villages grew quickly. By 1877 there were five furnaces at Quarter Ironworks employing almost 700 men and boys. The coal and ironstone mines were thriving and with them, the villages continued to grow. Before the ironworks was built, Limekilnburn had been the larger of the two villages, perhaps because of its location on a main route. The 1851 census shows a grocer and a toll house at Limekilnburn. The other toll house on that road was at Eddlewood, by Hamilton, about two miles away.

Before the Education Act of 1873, a school was set up in Darngaber by Colin Dunlop. It can only be supposed that it was for his workers' children, for no records survived from that early school. The log book of Quarter Public School for the week ending 9 April, 1877, mentioned that they had "Left school and marched across to the new buildings". Up until then the school had been held in a hall, built in 1857, on the other side of the road. The log book has a wealth of information about what life was like. The boys who were working there were expected to attend the old school hall for some education. The school was run during the evenings and was called "Quarter Evening Continuation School". The log book contains comments about the attendance on 25 October, 1894. "Numbers present this week not so good as a number are on night shift." The miners' strike in April and May of 1874 is mentioned. Families were "ejected from their houses".

The school log book also records the setting up of soup kitchens at the school during the strikes to try and feed the children of the miners. The entry for May, 1921 records that 200 children were receiving soup and bread at mid-day. They also received "tea and bread and butter" before they went home. The strike affected the school's finances, too. The penny each child had to pay to attend school was not often brought.

The strike of 1874 was not the first to affect the miners of the area. In 1862, they had gone on strike because the mine owners wanted to reduce their wages. The strike was broken when 5,000 miners in Lanarkshire were locked out to prevent them supporting the striking miners.

There was another strike in 1864, when the Quarter Ironworks workers came out in support of other employees of Colin Dunlop, at Clyde Ironworks near Glasgow, who had gone on strike for a pay rise of one shilling per day. The strike collapsed in Quarter when the miners were threatened with eviction from their company-owned houses.

In 1874 the demand for iron and coal was greatly reduced. 450 men from Quarter decided to strike to try and stop a 20% reduction in wages, but the miners were forced to accept the owners' terms in the end.

There were strikes again in 1894 and 1921, each time about pay and productivity.

All the time the size of the village of Limekilnburn stayed very much the same, while the former village of Darngaber had become Quarter Ironworks' village and had more than doubled in size.

By 1871, Quarter had its own provision store, owned by Colin Dunlop. This shop supplied everything that a villager might need, including spirits which were sold from a small room at the rear of the building. The "truck" system was in operation. This meant that the owners could charge high prices, without competition. James Keir Hardie, later to become a politician in London, was working as a miner at Quarter. He and his father nearly lost their jobs over his mother's attempt to set up a rival store. Keir Hardie eventually lost his job at Quarter because he agitated against the working conditions of the miners.

It is said that the women would wait at the mine offices at the crossroads on pay day for their husbands to collect their wages. The money would then be spent in the village store, only to be collected again by the wages office, and given out to the next shift to be paid, and so it went around again.

The public house is still on the same site. At some time during this period it gained its strange name, "The Bully Inn". No one is sure how or why it was so called. Some say it was named after Bellerophon, the figure from Greek mythology who rode the winged horse, Pegasus, whose name had been adopted by a local mining company. The Irish born miners could not pronounce Bellerophon, so it became "The Bully Inn". Another

157

suggestion has been that it was named after HMS Bellerophon, the ship from which Napoleon surrendered in 1815.

The good railway links with Quarter brought men from Strathaven and Larkhall to work at the ironworks or the pits. They also would walk from the surrounding villages. By the mid 1800s, there was a large number of men from Ireland living in the village. The number was so great that part of Laigh Quarter was known as "Dublin". The Irish born miners, once established in the village, would bring brothers or cousins from their own towns and villages to work in the ironworks or pits and live as boarders in their houses.

The ironstone by Laigh Quarter ran out in 1902 and the ironworks was closed by Colin Dunlop. The coal mining continued as part of the United Collieries group. At this time there were six working coal mines in and around Quarter. The site of the old iron works now became the "bing" – the dumping area for the waste coal.

At the turn of the century the working and living conditions of the miners were so poor that, in 1910, the Duchess Nina, wife of Alfred, thirteenth Duke of Hamilton, had built for the miners at Quarter an Institute to try to raise their standard of living. The building was opened with great celebration with many of the local dignitaries in attendance.

The Duchess Nina Miners' Institute was the first of many to be built in the area. It supplied many of the things missing in the village. It provided the equivalent of pit head baths for the miners. There was a reading room and library, a billiard room, carpet bowls, a shooting range and a meeting room with a kitchen attached. A skittle alley doubled as a summer ice rink for curling. The Duchess Nina even provided a bowling green next door. The miners formed a brass band. It was very modern for the time, being lit by electricity supplied from Quarter Colliery.

The village minister was eager that there should be places for the miners and their families to go in the evening other than the pub. The villagers had interests outside Quarter, taking the train to the races at Hamilton and supporting the football team, Quarter Huttonbank. The winter months meant curling on a flooded field by Limekilnburn at Airy Bog. During this period the communities saw their lives change. The village of Quarter, as you approached it from Limekilnburn, had a fine church and manse, a police house and two policemen, and at the other end of the village a grand Institute with many modern facilities. Limekilnburn had changed very little, as had Laigh Quarter, with most of the men working in the local pits.

Miners' Rows, Laigh Quarter

No 7 Pit, Quarter Colliery

During 1921, there were three pit closures when the coal seams in the lower levels were exhausted. The miners began to move away to other mines and other industries after the strike in that year. Number One pit at Laigh Quarter and Number Four pit at the crossroads in Quarter were the only ones working at that time.

The increasing mechanisation of the coal industry and a drop in the demand for coal were the beginning of the slow decline of the mining industry in the area. The Quarter miners joined the General Strike of 1926. The school log book again mentions the soup kitchens. It also mentions the children being examined for malnutrition. The onset of winter snow forced some of them to stay away from school because they had no boots to wear.

The miners and their families filled their time during that summer with football matches and galas for the children. Food was provided in part by the soup kitchens and part by the miners' ingenuity in growing their vegetables in the gardens. The soup kitchens were set up in the wash houses that lay behind the miners' rows. The huge water boilers were used to make the soup in. The pit ponies enjoyed an unexpected holiday that summer, having been brought to the surface and left to graze in a field in the village of Quarter. The pit ponies at Quarter, and later Knowetop, were the last ponies working underground in Scotland. They were still being used until the 1960s.

The very basic housing provided by Colin Dunlop's company in the 1850s was being changed and upgraded all the time. The "divots" (earth roofs) were replaced with a straw or thick thatch, then eventually by a slate roof. Wash houses were built behind the miners' rows. A group of twelve to fifteen dwellings would share a wash house, so it would be possible for a housewife to do her washing every two weeks. The key to the wash house was passed on to each family in turn. This system lasted well into the 1950s.

During the years of the Second World War the miners played a major role in the survival of the country's economy. Not all the men stayed at home, although mining was a reserved profession. Children were evacuated to Quarter from Glasgow for safety, a shock for some of the inner city children arriving in a small rural village.

The coal industry was nationalised in 1946 by which time there were only two working mines in Quarter. It was estimated that there was only another ten years' life left in these mines. They supported many of the families of the two villages. The houses had not changed much. Electricity had only been introduced in 1934, provided by the coal driven generator at the mine offices, and the main sewerage system had not yet reached the villages. There was a slow gradual population drift away from the area and by 1957 there were probably only 225 people left in Quarter and 90 in Limekilnburn.

The decision was made by the local authority to rehouse the people of Laigh Quarter, Quarter and Limekilnburn in a new housing scheme in nearby Eddlewood. This would leave Limekilnburn with a population of four and Quarter with thirty nine. This decision was taken because of the derelict condition of the houses, the lack of an adequate sewerage system and the falling population. At the time it seemed a peculiar decision as the villages had a popular primary school, a village store, a church, opened in 1884, and a pub. Those that had already moved to the new scheme still sent their children to the school, and worshipped in the village church. If the community was moved to the new scheme, a new school, church and store would have to be built.

The publicity that followed was enough to secure the future of the two villages. Because of the distance of Laigh Quarter from the main road, it was decided to move everyone from there to either Quarter or Eddlewood. Limekilnburn changed very little. Having mains electricity and sewerage made life very much easier. Many of the derelict houses in Quarter were demolished to make way for a council-built housing scheme to rehouse the remaining Quarter villagers. The rest of the houses were razed to the ground.

What had been dubbed a dying village was reborn in the form of modern bungalows along each side of the road, now named Limekilnburn Road. Quarter has now become a very popular place in which to live. The village over the intervening years has grown slowly, with quiet cul-de-sacs and large red brick houses. A few of the original houses remain, the white-washed "nurse's home" paid for by the miners from their meagre wages, the mine offices, now the offices of a tractor hire farm, and the school house, still occupied by teachers.

The Duchess Nina Institute closed in the 1950s. It had been used for many other things over the years and eventually became derelict. It lay open to the weather for a long time and was a pitiful sight. It is now a nursing home, restored nearly to its former glory. The one large monument to the history of the area is the bing or waste heap. It greets visitors as they enter the village of Quarter from Hamilton. The bing is not as large as it once was, and is being removed by degrees for infills for motorways and other things. These villages are not what they seem, small quiet back waters. They still have a strong sense of community.

COLIN'S HOT BLAST

The following is an extract from a much longer poem which appeared in "The Hamilton Advertiser" on 2 August, 1862. It celebrated the erection of furnaces at Quarter by Colin Dunlop and Co. of the Clyde Iron Works. The "mine" to which reference is made in the last verse is the technical name given to the calcined ironstone, when put into the furnace.

We bodies roun' Quarter may lift up our heads,
For we've gotten licht now to blazon our deeds;
We sat in the shadow for many a year past,
But now we're enlightened by Colin's hot blast!

Amang mineral men we've a standin' and name,
And for coal and pig-iron a far-carried fame-
With Gartsherrie, Dundyvan, an' Clyde we are classed,
Aye since the erection of Colin's hot blast!

The inventions brought out in this wonderful age
Will form a bright era on history's page;
Of the many inventions not one has surpassed
The ingenious contrivance of Colin's hot blast!

Tho' our corn-fields and pastures are blacken'd by smoke
And our sheep and horned cattle assume a dark coat
Yet meal, milk and butter are held in request
By the gudewives wha dwell near to Colin's hot blast!

The production of limestone, of coal, and of mine,
Cause a great circulation of guid British coin;
To the sons of industry its import is vast
'Tis a great public benefit, Colin's hot blast!

A.H.

THE STORY OF COAL MINING IN HAMILTON DISTRICT

Robert A. Clark and Sharon A. Martin

Hamilton in the 1990s looks, sounds and smells very different from how it was at the end of the Victorian age. Today, it is a town of high technology and service industries, proud of its motorway links to Glasgow and Edinburgh, and with growing importance as a centre for tourism and leisure. A century ago, Hamilton lay at the heart of Lanarkshire's coal mining industry and was a prosperous, though hardly beautiful, town of colliery headgears, smoking chimneys and miners' rows, criss-crossed by railways taking coal to the factories and blast furnaces, and to customers all over the world.

Coal mining in Hamilton had a rapid rise, and almost as quick a fall. Between about 1870 and the early 1930s, the mines probably employed more people than any other single industry. They brought jobs for many and wealth for a few. When they closed, the pit-bings and abandoned railway embankments stayed as scars on the landscape that will take centuries to heal. The remains of the mines are there to find if you want – the unexplained open area in a housing scheme that was the site of Fairhill Colliery, the line of the railway cutting under Low Waters Road that led to Cadzow Colliery, the contours of the land around Bent Sports Ground that outline the old bing for Bent Colliery, the remains of the winding engine houses for Whistleberry Colliery built into the modern brickworks, and many more. Even the River Clyde has traces of Lanarkshire's mining past, with a thick layer of black silt lying on the bottom, the result of the processes once used to clean the coal.

Nature did not lay down the seams of coal conveniently to match the boundaries of modern towns and villages. To understand the history of mining in Hamilton one must look at a much larger area, running from Blantyre to Stonehouse, west from the River Calder at East Kilbride, and east across into Motherwell and Clydesdale. There were a number of mines operating in Lanarkshire before 1700, but these were small pits working the coal where it came to the surface at places like Rutherglen, Quarter, the valleys of the Calder and Avon, and to the north over into Monklands. Between 1700 and 1800, output of coal rose four-fold, until by 1800 Lanarkshire was Scotland's most important mining area.

In the area we now think of as the town of Hamilton, the first mines were on the Duke of Hamilton's lands at Quarter, which produced small quantities of coal for local use. By the early nineteenth century, the Duke had his own mine at Avonbanks, near Chatelherault, which provided coal for the fires in Hamilton Palace. Like all these early mines, it was quite small and employed only a few men. The 1841 census for Hamilton shows that, from a population of 10,862, only ninety one worked in the mines. At Quarter Colliery, for example, between November 1835 and November 1836, the entire workforce consisted of a salesman, an engineman, two cleeksmen (who ran the haulage systems), a bottomer, a pony driver, a weigher and between fifteen and twenty eight hewers (Hamilton Estate Papers).

If one were to mark on a map the locations of these early mines, they would almost encircle the town of Hamilton. This was because it was not until nearly 1860 that the first pits were sunk beneath the town. There were two reasons for this. Although by the middle of the nineteenth century test borings had proved that there was coal both under the town and under the Duke of Hamilton's estates, for many years neither the Town Council nor the Duke would allow mining below their lands in or near the town. The second, and perhaps more important, explanation is, however, the geology of the area. In what is known as the "Hamilton Basin", which runs roughly from Blantyre to Quarter and from Earnock to the River Clyde at Motherwell, the coal seams lie under a thick layer of orangey-red sandstone, up to a thousand feet thick in places, which was known as "the "barren red measures". The cost and practical difficulty of sinking deep shafts through the barren red measures, which in places are waterlogged, meant that it was at best uneconomic, and at worst impossible, to reach the coal. Furthermore, up until the mid-nineteenth century, the local demand for coal could be met from the existing shallow mines at places like Quarter and Avonbanks.

All this changed between the 1830s and the 1870s. Demand for coal was increasing rapidly, to fuel Lanarkshire's developing ironmaking industry. A single blast furnace needed at least 5,000 tons of coal each year, and it was estimated that, by 1796, the industry had an annual requirement of about 90,000 tons. At the same time, other industries were developing and creating the demand for coal: glassmaking, brewing, distilling, sugar refining and heavy engineering, as well as domestic fuel for the growing towns, particularly in the growth areas of Glasgow and Edinburgh.

Railways crept south from Glasgow and north from Carlisle, providing cheap and quick transport for Lanarkshire coal to markets opening up locally and all over central Scotland, and eventually throughout the world. Most of the easily mined shallow coal had gone, but the application of new scientific understanding to mining engineering, and improvements to the equipment available – particularly for the sinking of shafts – created the circumstances where new mines could be sunk through the barren red measures to reach the coal below. Demand provided the impetus, and the availability of cheap railway transport and better techniques of mining provided the means: between 1871 and 1877, fourteen collieries with thirty two pits opened within a two mile radius of Hamilton West railway station.

The first to begin working the Hamilton coal was the Duke. His specialist advisers could see the possibility of large profits from the coal under his estates. From the early 1850s, he agreed to allow the development of new, large-scale mines, initially on his lands between Ferniegair and Larkhall. Merryton Colliery opened in 1856, Allanton Colliery in 1862, and Home Farm and Bog Collieries by 1865.

The first mine to open in what is now the town of Hamilton was Greenfield Colliery at Burnbank, in 1859. This was developed by James Nisbet, at the time Provost of the Burgh, on land leased from Mr Lewis Potter. The Town Council was, however, reluctant to allow mining under its own lands, and took from 1838 to 1874 to decide its coal could be worked. Even Provost Nisbet could not persuade the reluctant Councillors to permit mining when, in 1860, he asked them for a lease.

Until Nationalisation in 1947, when ownership of coal reserves moved to the government, it was generally the landowner who held the mineral rights. Originally, the crown owned all the minerals below ground, but this was challenged in the reign of Queen Elizabeth I, and thereafter it was accepted that the landowner had rights to all the minerals below his land except gold and silver, which remained with the crown. The landowner had the right to lease, or "set in tack", his mineral rights, for profit. After the Union in 1707, this precedent was extended to Scotland.

Throughout the period between 1850 and 1900, many Lanarkshire land owners signed leases with specialist mining companies who paid royalties on the coal mined. These companies, such as William Barr & Sons, (Allanton and Merryton Collieries), Hamilton, McCulloch & Co. (Home Farm and Bog Collieries), worked the coal and sold it on to the

market. Some landowners, such as John Watson, owner of Earnock House, opened mines themselves. In a number of cases, leases were also taken by iron manufacturing companies, keen to ensure a constant supply of coal for their furnaces. An example of this was the mines at Quarter, owned by Colin Dunlop & Co.

For a town that has almost forgotten its coal-dust stained past, it is worth listing some of the major mines and when they opened, the sites of which have disappeared under today's housing schemes, industrial estates and roads: Allanshaw (opened 1874), Bent (1873), Cadzow (1876), Clyde (1874), Earnock (1874), Eddlewood (1874), Fairhill (by 1880), Ferniegair (by 1860), Greenfield (1859), Hamilton Palace (1884), Haughhead (1867), Neilsland (by 1890), Ross (1883), Silverton (1875), Townsland (1876), Udston (1877) and Wellhall (1874). This process was being mirrored in the surrounding area. In Blantyre, there was Auchinraith (1879), Bardykes (by 1900), Blantyreferme (by 1900), Blantyre (1873), Craighead (by 1879) and Whistleberry (1894). Around Larkhall, there was Ashgill (by 1900), Canderrigg (by 1900), Cornsilloch (by 1879), South Longrigg (by 1900) and Swinhill (by 1900). At Bothwell and Uddingston, there was Bothwell Castle (by 1879), Bothwell Park (by 1879) and Clydeside (by 1900). The last mine to open in the Hamilton Basin was at Whistleberry, on the boundary between Blantyre and Hamilton, which was sunk in 1894 to reach the coal under the Auchinraith Estate owned, until his death in 1893, by a former Provost of Hamilton, Colonel John Clark Forrest.

In comparison with elsewhere in Britain, many of these mines were quite small. Typically, they employed between one hundred and two hundred and fifty men underground, and perhaps fifty on the surface, where the coal was sorted by size, cleaned and loaded. Some surface workers were employed as engineers, blacksmiths, locomotive drivers, clerks, and so on, all of whom were necessary to keep the mine working. There were, however, some larger mines: Bent, Cadzow, Greenfield and Neilsland all employed at their peak seven or eight hundred men. The two biggest mines in the area were Earnock Colliery, opened in 1874, and Hamilton Palace Colliery. This was developed as a second mine by the Bent Colliery Co. Ltd from 1884, but eventually became larger than its parent and indeed outlasted it. We are fortunate in having a mass of detail from the early years of these mines. The letter book from Hamilton Palace Colliery between November 1884 and November 1889, and the "daybook", or diary, from Earnock Colliery between

1877 and 1890, survive in the local museum collections.

Both in their way were pioneering mines. History acknowledges that Earnock was the first mine in the world to use electric lights underground, and was a model of mining excellence. The daybook for Earnock records how, on 19th April, 1883, the manager, James Gilchrist, "got instructions from Mr Watson to arrange for extension of Electric Plant so that Earnock House may be lit by Swans Incandescent Lamps". The book unfortunately does not record when the new installation was complete, but it is possible that the Hamilton coal owner, John Watson, was the first person in Scotland to have his house lit by electricity.

The letter book from Hamilton Palace Colliery gives us a wealth of detail about the day-to-day workings of a developing late Victorian coal mine: orders for seal oil for the mining lamps, tender specifications for the construction of the pit rows, an application to the Duke's factor for land for a football pitch for the miners, formal notification to the Mines Inspector of a collier prosecuted for having matches underground, complaints about faults with the winding engine bought from the firm of Grant, Ritchie & Co. at Kilmarnock, and the delivery of too much gunpowder. An ongoing saga played out over several years was the pioneering purchase from a mine in Coventry, England, of first one, then a second, coal-cutting machine for making the roadways in areas of coal being developed for extraction.

A Dangerous Calling

Mining has always been a dangerous industry, and the annual reports of the Mines Inspector from the end of the last century record a catalogue of deaths and injuries in Lanarkshire mines, including many from the Hamilton area. The natural hazards of roof falls and gas – both the explosive *firedamp* (methane) and the suffocating *blackdamp* (mainly carbon dioxide) – were augmented by the dangers of working machinery in confined spaces. Surface workmen regularly fell down shafts, as did *shankers*, the men who looked after the shafts themselves. *Brushers*, who maintained the underground roadways, regularly blew themselves up by using too much gunpowder or were crushed by falling stones. Everyone, particularly the boy pony-drivers, suffered the threat of being caught between or under railway wagons or their smaller-size equivalent, "hutches", used underground.

Men who survived uninjured rarely worked beyond middle age, and for many years it was the case that a man who could not work faced the threat of eviction for him and his family from the house provided by the mine owners. For the colliers actually on the coal-face, the natural and man-made dangers were made worse by the pressure created by wages being tied directly to their output. The priority of owners and management was maximum production at cheapest cost, with the safety of the workforce coming a very poor second.

If accidents and deaths were common, the mines in Hamilton were fortunately spared the horrors which affected other areas, particularly Blantyre. The list of Britain's major mining disasters records only one in Hamilton, which took place on 28 May 1887, at Udston Colliery. At 9.05 am, an explosion ripped through the workings in the Splint seam, killing seventy-three men and boys. "Traces of the extreme violence of the explosion were visible through all the Splint coal workings .... the shock was felt in the workings of Greenfield Colliery through a barrier of solid coal 45 yards thick" (Mines Inspectors Report). The Mines Inspector concluded that the explosion had been caused by unauthorised shotfiring, probably by one of two brothers, both of whom died in the explosion. It was then quite common for miners to "fire shots" to blast down the coal themselves, although this was illegal, rather than stand idle waiting for an official to come and do it for them. The flame from the shot ignited a pocket of gas, which then set off a rolling fireball fuelled by the dry coal dust covering everything in the mine.

When investigating the accident, the Mines Inspector was much troubled by the fact that the amount of firedamp in the mine was not sufficient to explain the force and size of the explosion. His conclusion that a small gas explosion had triggered a larger coal dust explosion drew on contemporary scientific research proving that coal dust can explode as violently as gas. Many of the large mine disasters of the Victorian period – including that at Blantyre in 1877 which killed more than 200 people – are now thought to have been caused more by dust than by gas. The Udston disaster was the first accident where dust was officially recognised as the cause.

Mining Geology in Hamilton

There were considerable quantities of coal under Hamilton. **Economic Geology of the Central Coalfield of Scotland**, published in 1920, gives full geological details. Excluding a number of seams only a few inches thick which were ignored everywhere, twelve main seams of coal were worked in Hamilton, although none of the mines worked all of them.

In some places only three or four of the thicker seams were ever worked.

Although all coal is black and burns, every seam is slightly different in its exact chemical composition, and mining engineers and scientists classify coal according to what it can best be used for. Thus, in the past, some seams were "House Coal", others "Steam Coal", others "Gas Coal", "Coking Coal", "Furnace Coal", and so on. The thickness of each seam was not constant – even in one mine, a seam might vary from nine inches to five feet thick. The thickness of rock between the seams varied from a hundred feet or more to just a couple of feet and, to confuse things further, this also varied, so that in one colliery two seams might be sixty feet apart, and in another have only a few feet between them, allowing the two to be mined together. Each seam had its own name, and now that mining in Hamilton has ceased entirely it is worth remembering what these were.

The first workable seam to be reached under the barren red measures was the *Upper*, which was not often mined. Below that was the *Ell*, so called because in the area's earliest pits the seam was generally about one ell thick (the ell was a traditional Scottish unit of measurement not much used after the eighteenth century). The Ell was one of the main targets of many of the mines – the Earnock Colliery daybook for 16th September 1878, recorded in triumph that No. 2 shaft had "reached the Ell Coal at a depth of 118 fathoms" (mineshaft depths were traditionally measured in fathoms rather than feet and yards).

Below the Ell is a seam of ironstone – a form of iron ore – once mined and smelted locally. This contains a mass of fossilised mussel shells, and was thus known as the *Musselband Ironstone*. In places, it is hard and polishes well to make an attractive ornamental finish, which gave the seam its nickname of *Cambuslang Marble*. A fireplace surround made of this can be seen in the Duke of Hamilton's eighteenth century Banqueting Hall at Chatelherault, south of Hamilton.

Next in sequence is the *Pyotshaw*, a furnace coal, and below that the *Main*, used as house coal. This was, after the Ell, perhaps the most important target for a mine owner. This was followed by the *Humph* coal, and then by the *Splint*, a very hard seam often five feet or more thick, ideally suited for use in blast furnaces because it could be extracted in large blocks which would withstand the pressure of a furnace without breaking up into small pieces and thus choking the draught. The Splint was a particularly important seam, and indeed one could say that the prosperity of Hamilton's mines was based more than anything on just three main seams – the Ell, the Main and the Splint. Below the Splint is the *Virgin*, a house coal, and below that in turn the *Blackband*, the *Virtuewell*, the *Kiltongue*, a steam coal, the *Upper Drumgray* and the *Lower Drumgray*. In some places, the Upper and the Lower Drumgray seams come together as one.

Mining in the Hamilton Basin was never easy. Many of the seams are hard and relatively thin and, in the millions of years after the coal was formed, the area went through a series of violent geological upheavals. The whole coalfield is very badly faulted where, in past ages, whole areas of rock several miles square have been thrust up or pushed down anything from a few inches to more than six hundred feet. Mine plans for the area show how the miners were constantly having to work through faults, exploring upwards or downwards to find the seam. Another problem was the effect of volcanic activity – millions of years in the past, but still millions of years after the coal was formed. Many mine plans show areas described as "Want", where the coal had been burned away and replaced by a lava flow that might be a hundred yards or more wide. Finally, many of the Lanarkshire coal seams slope steeply, making it difficult both to win the coal in the first place, and then to get it out of the mine. In the end, it was mainly these difficult geological conditions which brought about the end of coal mining in Hamilton.

The End of an Era

By 1900, no major new mines were being developed, and indeed some of those which had been the first to open and which had particularly difficult conditions or had been mining under a relatively small area, had closed by the outbreak of the First World War. One of the first to go was Allanshaw Colliery. Cited in mining textbooks from the 1880s as a model example of how to work the Lanarkshire seams, it had closed by 1911. Other early closures were Townsland, at Hamilton West, and Wellhall, near Burnbank. The British mining industry hit its peak of production in 1913 and, in 1914, with the outbreak of the First World War, quickly got into difficulties as the chaos of war and the threat of German U-boats vastly reduced the export market. Wartime needs for munitions kept up the demand for a while, but when peace came in 1919, the bottom dropped out of the market and collieries started closing.

Throughout the 1920s, Hamilton's mines shut one by one. In some cases, mines were merged, but even these merged mines did not last long. In the early 1930s, the Great Depression that struck industry throughout the western world had a drastic impact on Hamilton's coalmines and, by 1935, few collieries remained. When the coal industry was nationalised in 1947, only a handful of pits remained. Hamilton Palace Colliery enjoyed a brief prominence in the 1950s, taking out the remaining coal from under the site of Hamilton Palace and the Low Parks, but it, too, closed in 1959. Some new small, short-life drift mines, known as "in-gaun e'es" (in going eyes), were opened in the 1950s, to reach areas of shallow coal on the high ground between Quarter, Ferniegair and Larkhall. Avonbraes, Beaton's Lodge and Knowetop were some of the sites. The last to shut, in the early 1960s, were at Quarter, where mining had first started in Hamilton centuries before.

Mining in Hamilton since the 1960s has been restricted to a few small opencast sites around the town, where modern quarrying methods have been used to extract the thin seams which could not be worked economically in the past, and the coal left in the thicker seams by our forebears' inefficient mining methods. There may be more of these sites in the years to come, but there is no doubt that Hamilton must consign to history its brief heyday as a centre of a booming coal-mining industry.

MINER'S MORNING SONG

Arise! brother miner! 'Twas only a dream,
That hum of green woodlands, that stroll by the stream;
Some joy-loving fairy, in portraiture gay,
Hath shown thee by night what thou sees not by day.
Yet, brother, despair not; the hours will pass o'er;
We'll rise, as the day wanes, to gladness once more.

Suppress those deep sighs, brother, though it may be
The fate of thy kinsman is waiting for thee:
O'er sorrows untasted 'tis folly to brood;
We must, like that kinsman, brave danger for food.
Then up and be stirring; like serf-men of yore,
We'll rest when we've plodded our portion once more.

Be cheerful, poor brother! I've heard of a land
Where no over-labour e'er blisters the hand -
A land where no fetters of slavery are seen,
Where the grindstone of tyranny never hath been.
Perhaps we'll go there when our ploddings are o'er,
And then we'll be weary-boned miners no more.

David Wingate

STONEHOUSE

Stonehouse Heritage Group

Prehistoric Stonehouse

In prehistoric times, a natural place to settle would have been by the river Avon, with its abundance of fish and its nearby fertile grasslands. On a small mound, half a mile to the west of modern Stonehouse, it is believed there once stood the standing stones that gave the village its name. There still can be seen today three standing stones at Avonholm overlooking the Avon between Stonehouse and Glassford and it may well be that the word "Stanes" has in time been corrupted into the present Stonehouse. The stones are thought to have been a religious meeting place similar to our own churches, and the expression, "Let's go to the stanes", meaning "Let's go to church" survives to this day in some parts of Scotland.

The Romans

In 80 AD, Governor Gnaeus Julius Agricola led an army of 20,000 men into Scotland, establishing forts across Scotland, as far north as Angus. To supply their garrisons and to control the occupied territory, the Romans set about building a network of roads. A two kilometre stretch of this network can be seen at Dykehead in the form of a 0.5m high causeway. It is likely that the road was a supply route between Ayr and Edinburgh, passing through the forts at Castledykes and Allanton near Loudon Hill.

The Coming of Christianity

Christianity came to the area around 340 AD, when St Ninian of Candida Casa (Whithorn) reputedly built the first church in Stonehouse, probably on what was then the site of the standing stones and is now the old kirk graveyard. This leads us to another possibility for the origins of the name Stonehouse, for the old kirk graveyard was built on a mound or "knowe", giving rise to a possible derivation of "Stone Knowe".

Although the first church could have been constructed from wood like the early dwelling houses, it may have been a stone building, leading to yet another theory concerning the origins of the village's name, for

177

it was common to call towns after the first stone building erected there, which was more often than not a church. Whatever the answer to the mystery surrounding the origins of the village and its name, Stonehouse is a parish steeped in history.

Early Stonehouse

Several castles or tower houses existed within the boundaries of Stonehouse. Cot, Cat or Coat Castle existed on a precipitous cliff face to the south of the village, near the banks of the river Avon. The basic tower house was either a square or rectangular building, rising through three or more stories and enclosing a hall, chamber, kitchen, chapel and final place of refuge. Cot Castle was probably very similar to the tower house within Craignethan Castle which is thought to date to the fifteenth century. In the early nineteenth century, lime kilns were opened on the ruins of Cot Castle in connection with the extraction of the lime which was abundant in the area. All that remains now are two lime kilns set into the bank with spherical arched draw holes and projecting buttresses. Cot Castle Farm was later built on this site but fell into disrepair and was abandoned at the end of the 1970s.

Ringsdale was another tower house standing high on the Avon Gorge overlooking the winding river beneath. The name may derive from the ancient language of the Britons, Rhyn signifying a promontory or hill. Today, all that remains of the castle are large stone blocks which have fallen from the summit of the gorge to the river banks. An 1838 map shows that at one time a mill known as Cloxy Mill stood near the remains of Ringsdale Castle, though today there are no visible signs of its existence or any records of its origins.

Apart from the two castles mentioned above, Bleau's map of 1596 shows a Kemp Castle on the site more commonly known as Castlehill and two 'Kat Castles', one being the present castle located at the head of Strathaven Road and the second in the region of High Longridge (Langrigg) farm.

Religion

By 400 AD Christianity had become the official religion of the Roman Empire. Around the middle of the fourth century, a man called Ninian was born near the Solway and was later converted to Christianity. He travelled to Rome and after a period of study moved to France to continue his instruction in Christianity, which it was his ultimate goal to bring to his homeland of Scotland. Legend tells that he brought earth from "Candida Casa" (house of white stone) and, with his monks, scattered this on the ancient burial grounds of pagan worship such as the "stanes" of Stonehouse. (It is believed that some of the sacred earth was taken from Stonehouse to consecrate the grounds of the Glassford Kirk cemetery, the present day remains of which are almost identical to those of St Ninian's churchyard in Stonehouse.) It is likely that a church stood on the site at Stonehouse from that time onwards, and in the ninth century, the old kirk was dedicated to St Ninian.

A number of men and women from Stonehouse parish were Covenanters or connected with the movement. James Thomson, a farmer from Tanhill, died from wounds received at the Battle of Drumclog in 1679 and was later interred in St Ninian's churchyard. Margaret Law or Nisbet of Loudon, near Drumclog, sustained her family whilst they were fugitives after the Battle of Bothwell Bridge, finally succumbing to starvation and ill-health in 1683. Her husband, John Nisbet, returned from hiding to find not only his wife but also his daughter had died. Grief-stricken, he carried his daughter's body all the way to Stonehouse churchyard and buried her beside her mother. He was later captured at a prayer meeting in Fenwick and was executed in Edinburgh in 1685. These and many other brave men and women suffered and died for their devoutly held beliefs.

All that remains today of Stonehouse's old St Ninian's Church is the gable end of a pre-reformation church and its bell tower. Reference is made to the old kirk in documentary evidence from the late seventeenth century. In 1772, a contemporary writer recorded that "the church was rebuilt," although it is not certain whether this was to replace the decaying Old St Ninian's at the glebe or whether there was already a church on the site of what is today described as the Old Parish Church, now used as a wholesale cash-and-carry. In 1894, because of the lack of space, a new church was opened, which in 1929, after the Union of the Churches, was renamed St Ninian's Parish Church of Scotland.

The first Free Church was built in 1843 and was in use until 1874 when a new church, with a 117 foot spire, was opened. Following the amalgamation of the Hamilton Memorial Church and St Ninian's, there was found to be no need for two churches, and the demolition of the Free Church building began in 1954.

The first church for the Associates Secession or Burgher

denomination was built in 1796. It remained in use until 1878 and, in 1879, the present structure was erected, originally called the United Free Church and later becoming the Paterson Church, in honour of the Reverend H A Paterson, the church's minister until his death in 1901.

A Salvation Army Hall stood in Kirk Street until the 1950s, later moving to the top of Wellbrae.

Holy Wells

Scotland has an abundance of holy wells and Stonehouse is no exception. Four holy wells are found within the parish and numerous others supply the needs of the village. Holy wells are of pagan origin, from a time when there were many superstitions surrounding water. Pilgrims from all over the surrounding country would flock to try their healing properties or administer Christian baptisms, as was probably the case at St. Ninian's well.

St. Ninian's well, like the old kirk church and churchyard, was dedicated to St. Ninian. It has over the centuries been corrupted into Ringan well and to Ring well but today all that remains is a marshy area of grass in which cows now graze, between the farm of Eastmains and the old kirk.

Situated on the banks of the Avon on the lands of Patrickholm lies St. Patrick's well, famous for its healing properties in curing tuberculosis and skin diseases. It may be coincidental but Stonehouse Hospital was opened in 1896 to provide care and treatment for sufferers of tuberculosis and other related diseases. This well, like so many others, was dedicated to another preacher of Christianity. St. Patrick is said to have spread the gospel throughout this area including Dalserf and, like Ninian, his name appears throughout the country. This sulphurous spring can still be seen today, trickling through a stratum of rock and cascading down the gorge.

St. Anthony's well was a prominent well in its time. It was also known as Brackenhill well, situated not a great distance from Spittal House which was formerly a hospital and a convent, built in 1723. According to the dictionary definition, "spittal" or "spittle", was a hospital for foul diseases. The site of the well can still be found today surrounded by a small stone wall. Unfortunately, through vandalism and boring during the New Town survey, the well has long since dried up. It is thought that Anthony came from a wealthy family and spoke only his native language, which was that of the ancient Egyptians. He was known as the carer of the poor, patron and protector of the lower animals. The well which was dedicated to him was notable for being high in iron content and known for curing diseases, particularly those of horses. It was believed that horses were taken to drink at the spring and sometimes the water was carried a considerable distance for healing purposes.

St. Laurence's well rises from the Watstonburn at Chapel where an ancient chapel was formerly built, dedicated to St. Laurence, the guardian of this well. Little is known of his well or its medicinal powers. St. Laurence himself was called the deacon and martyr of Rome, carer of the destitute, helpless and sick. All of these wells may have been sacred as late as the medieval era.

Weavers

During the seventeenth, eighteenth and the early nineteenth centuries, Stonehouse expanded as a weaving community specialising in silk production. Silk weaving took considerable skill and training as well as more complex equipment, whereas other fabrics were more easily produced and less skill was needed. The numbers employed in the industry in Stonehouse steadily grew from 131 in 1792 to 400 in 1841, rising to a peak of 500 in 1891. Handloom weaving was very much a family business, the trade being handed down from father to son. The women, too, were involved in pin winding, tambouring and embroidery. At the latter end of the nineteenth century, the introduction of the Jacquard handloom changed the style of weaving dramatically by enabling the weaver to produce several intricate patterns.

The Stonehouse weavers got their materials from agents in the village as well as from Strathaven and Larkhall. These agents included Thomas Frew of Queen Street, Strathaven; Caldwell and Young of King Street, Stonehouse and Robert Miller of Camnethan Street, Stonehouse. During the mid nineteenth century, two friendly societies were providing sickness relief for weavers. As power loom weaving increased, the handloom weavers could not compete with the prices of cotton, woollen and linen materials due to those materials being bought in larger quantities. Despite the decline, Stonehouse weavers established a reputation in the craft of silk hand weaving which continued until the demand for silk material dropped after the Great War. As the pay became poor and work scarce, the weavers had gradually over the latter end of the nineteenth century turned to work in agriculture or the mines to supplement their income. Some continued working, in Hamilton, Larkhall, Stonehouse and Strathaven. For the outlying villagers, before the days of the railway, it meant a long walk. The silk loom belonging to Robert and James Hamilton of Camnethan Street, the last two weavers in Lanarkshire, can now be seen in the Royal Scottish Museum, Edinburgh.

When weaving was at its peak in the early 1800s, the weavers were prosperous enough to own their own property. Streets of privately owned cottages were built, such as those in Hill Road. The houses were usually one storey terraced buildings with the front door opening onto the street. This door led to a stone-flagged entry which gave access to the weaving shop on one side and to the living quarters of one or two rooms on the other. A ladder from the entry to the loft gave storage and extra sleeping space, and a wash house was usually added at the rear of the building. The weaving shop would hold from one to four looms, worked by the weaver and his family. The first of these houses cost between £45 and £60, with the repayments being only a little more than the cost of rent.

The main diet of the weavers was potatoes, oatmeal, buttermilk and salted fish. There was a great dependence on potatoes, especially during the nineteenth century. Oatmeal, however, remained more important in their diet than bread or potatoes despite the cheapness of bread and the difficulties in preparing oatmeal. Milk, particularly in the form of buttermilk, was also popular while, instead of meat, herring or salt ling were consumed. Tea, sugar, butter, salt and meat were considered luxuries. Many Stonehouse weavers used the space at the back of cottages to grow vegetables to supplement their diet.

Sanitation was primitive. There were no sewers. Ordinary houses had no toilets - not even outdoor toilets. All they had was a bucket or a chamber pot which was kept underneath the bed or behind the door. When they were finished with it, it was emptied into the street. All the household rubbish was also thrown out into the street. Many houses had cess pits beside their front doors into which all the rubbish and excrement was emptied. The streets were like open sewers. If a town was fortunate, it would have "scavengers", the original dustmen, who went round the streets shovelling up rubbish and taking it to the town's midden. Due to the quantities of dung heaps and rubbish in the streets, vermin infestation (mice and rats) was common. People tried to keep their food out of the way in baskets hanging from the ceiling where the rodents had less chance of getting at it. Another effect was that the water supplies often became contaminated, causing typhoid and cholera.

In 1845, it was generally thought that the life expectancy of a man in the upper class was approximately forty seven years compared to twenty six for those at the bottom of the social ladder. One in four children died before they reached one year old. The young and old were particularly at risk. With little medical help or medicine available, they were vulnerable to many diseases such as typhus, measles, whooping cough, diphtheria and cholera. Inadequate nourishment and living conditions did nothing to confront the various ailments. Sleeping arrangements among the weavers exacerbated the spread of disease, particularly cholera outbreaks, as it proved almost impossible to isolate cases. Another factor which may have increased the weavers' vulnerability to disease was their liking for drink. In 1893, the parochial board met to consider the feasibility of erecting a fever hospital in the parish, and the resultant Stonehouse Hospital opened in 1896, said to be "the best isolation hospital in Scotland".

Trades and Industry

The geology of Stonehouse has provided the raw materials worked by the people of the community for centuries - sandstone, limestone, ironstone, shale, slate and coal. Around 1840, James Young developed the extraction of oil from shale, and this was worked near the Ritchies on the Avon, although no traces remain of the site.

The first railway lines in the village were laid to transport coal from the mines and it was the mines that provided most jobs after the decline of the weaving industry. In 1913, coal production peaked at 42 million tons, with a workforce of 148,000. The loss of the export trade after World War I, the emergence of alternative energy sources and industrial unrest in the 1920s, however, resulted in the decline of the industry. The Miners' Welfare Institute, built in 1924 for local miners, was sold to the District Council in 1956 for public use.

Another major employer from the mid eighteenth century to the First World War was Overwood sandstone quarry which supplied the stone for the construction of the Glasgow tenements and many important public and commercial buildings.

In 1836, a small company opened manufacturing candle wicks from

The Annual Parade, Stonehouse

cotton, and continued to trade until the 1950s. Another thriving employer in the nineteenth century was the tileworks at the bottom of Union Street. A second tile and brickworks existed in the 1950s at Greenburn. In addition to these major employers were the small occupational trades which supported the community - blacksmiths, millers, lime burners, publicans, shoemakers and so on.

After the Second World War, the parish became a fruit growing district, until competition from abroad put an end to this industry. Today, the major employer is Stonehouse Hospital.

Agriculture

In the early eighteenth century, corn and grass were extensively grown within the parish, and also flax, although production of the latter died out towards the end of the century. During the following century these were overtaken by oats, potatoes, turnips, beans and barley, although hay continued to be sold in large quantities. Cheese was also made in quantity until the mid nineteenth century but, with improvements to the railway network, milk was easier to transport and the cheese was produced elsewhere. In 1851, 30% of the male employed population worked directly in agriculture, more than in textiles and mining put together. By 1901, the percentage of male workers employed in farming had dropped to 14%, and there was a corresponding decline in the rural population as people moved to the cities and new jobs were created through industrialisation.

There are approximately fifty farms in the parish now, all dairy, and nearly all the land is arable.

Education

The earliest record of a school in Stonehouse parish dates to the beginning of the eighteenth century, although its whereabouts are uncertain. By 1780, a school stood close to the site of the present Townhead Street School, with the schoolmaster's house at 44 King Street. The school house was low roofed, ill ventilated and earth paved, but reasonably well attended. Beside the parochial school, there were others scattered around the parish, and by 1836, there were five schools, attended by nearly 300 scholars. Following the Education Act 1872, when education became state controlled and responsibility for the parish and burgh schools was transferred to school boards, the Stonehouse school board acquired Greenside School for infant education, the children later transferring to Camnethan Street or Townhead Street. The Free Kirk School in Hill Road opened in 1851.

Greenside School was latterly used as a school for woodwork and domestic sciences. Camnethan Street School was closed in 1947 and has been demolished to make way for a housing development. The children transferred to the Townhead Street School. Arising from the growth of the village since the Second World War, another school was needed and, in 1979, Newfield Primary School was opened.

Leisure

Curling has long been a popular winter sport in Stonehouse, played at the Tilework Park. In the summer, the favourite pastime of the weavers was kyles (a game using a large wooden ball and nine kyles or skittles), while the miners preferred quoits where a 10lb steel band was aimed at a vertical metal pin, eighteen or twenty one yards away. A bowling club was formed in 1857 at Loch Hall, later moving to the present location at Vicars Road. Other leisure pursuits during the nineteenth century were cricket, lawn tennis, cycling, golf, horse racing and football. Stonehouse continues to perform well on the football pitch, and Stonehouse Violet had its greatest success to date in 1978 when nearly the whole village turned out at Hampden Park to see them reaching the Junior Cup Final, sadly beaten 1-0 by Bonnyrigg Rose.

Modern Stonehouse

Stonehouse has always been a small, thriving, close-knit community, with many hard working organisations pulling together to provide the village with a variety of recreational pursuits and community support groups. It has the potential to expand and prosper, developing its industrial and residential capacity without altering its essential character. With the first phase of the bypass complete, the village can now look forward to a redeveloped centre within the conservation area, making Stonehouse an attractive place for potential residents and small business to locate themselves. Above all, we must endeavour to preserve our village's community spirit and character and provide our future generation with a sound economic base and healthy environment in which to live.

STONEHOUSE VIOLET

The following is an extract from a much longer poem
about the Stonehouse football team.

This nicht as by the fire I sit
Tae aulden times my fancies flit,
Tae that guid team a "fitba' dream"
The Stonehouse Violet fitba' team.

I can't just put a year upon it,
I've maybe gone " a wee bit daunert",
But still, the lads I mind sae weel
Wha's mair than ordnar fitba' skill.

The Junior gemmes, then, were a treat,
They aye had skill (an' sometimes meat),
They ne'er had heard o' "strikers", "sweepers",
But they'd educated feet, an' peepers.

The fitba noo, alas, alack,
I'm pretty sure the game's "gaun back",
Unless it's true what I'm whiles tauld
"Yer bluids gaun thin; ye're growin' auld".

William McCoubrey

BIBLIOGRAPHY

Suggestions for Further Reading

Hamilton District/Lanarkshire

British Geological Survey. *The Midland Valley of Scotland. British Regional Geology series, 3rd. edition by I.B. Cameron and D. Stephenson. (H.M.S.O., 1985)*

Lanarkshire: an inventory of the Prehistoric and Roman Monuments. (Royal Commission on the Ancient and Historical Monuments of Scotland, 1978)

Sinclair, Sir John. (ed.) *(Old) Statistical Account of Scotland 1791-1799. Vol. VII Lanarkshire and Renfrewshire. (EP Publishing, reprinted 1973)*

(New) Statistical Account of Lanarkshire. (William Blackwood and Sons, 1841)

Thomson, George. *(ed.) Third Statistical Account of Scotland. The County of Lanark. (Collins, 1960)*

Wilson, James Alexander. *A contribution to the history of Lanarkshire. 2 volumes.*
(J.Wylie and Co., 1936-37)

General sources such as the Statistical Accounts of Lanarkshire contain information on all towns and villages in Hamilton District and are recommended as a starting point for local history research.

Hamilton (including Quarter)

Griffen, Hugh. *Bygone Hamilton. (Stenlake and McCourt, 1990)*

Hamilton 1475-1975. (Burgh of Hamilton Quincentenary Committee, 1975)

Hamilton past and present. (Hamilton and District Civic Society, 1932)

Hamilton Town Council Minute Books 1701-1975.

Lochhead, Jessie H. *Hamilton in days gone by. (rev. ed., 1969)*

Miller, Alfred G. *Municipal Hamilton: a sketch of its institutions. (c.1890)*

Naismith's Hamilton Directory for 1878-79, including Bothwell, Blantyre, Uddingston, Motherwell and Larkhall, to which is added a history of Hamilton and neighbourhood. (W.Naismith, 1879)

A resource history of the church in Hamilton. (Hamilton Church History Project, 1987)

Stothers's guide to places of interest between Hamilton and Quarter. (Thomas Stothers, c.1910)

Torric, E.P.Dennison and Coleman, Russel. *Historic Hamilton. (Historic Scotland and Centre for Scottish Urban History, University of Edinburgh, due for publication 1995)*

Walker, Gavin. (comp.) *Victorian and Edwardian photographs of Hamilton District. (Hamilton District Libraries and Museum, 1979)*

Wallace, William. *Hamilton enterprise in retrospect. (Bell College, rev.ed., 1987)*

Hamilton Estates

Aspects of Scottish Classicism, the house and its formal setting 1690-1750. Proceedings of a Symposium held at Chatelherault, Hamilton, May 18th 1988. (St. Andrew's University and Blakeley Milroy, 1989)

Chatelherault M.S.C. Project Team. Cadzow Castle. (Unpublished report, 1985)

Marshall, Rosalind K. *The days of Duchess Anne: life in the household of the Duchess of Hamilton 1656-1716. (Collins, 1973)*

Paton, Sharon. *A fine house: the history of Mr. Crawford's house and offices 1696-1994. (Unpublished report, 1994)*

Walker, Gavin. *Hamilton Palace, a photographic record. (Hamilton District Libraries and Museum, 1976)*

Blantyre

Blantyre Local History Project. *A short history (of Blantyre). (Strathclyde Region Community Education Service, 1985)*

Cormack, Ian L. *Old Blantyre. (I.L.Cormack, 1988)*

Wright, Rev. Stewart. *Annals of Blantyre. (Wilson and McCormick, 1885)*

David Livingstone

Blaikie, William G. *The personal life of David Livingstone. (John Murray, 1880)*

Jeal, Tim. *Livingstone. (Heinemann, 1973)*

MacNair, James I. *Livingstone the liberator. (Collins, 1940)*

Livingstone, David. *Missionary travels and researches in South Africa. (John Murray, 1857)*

Livingstone, David. *Narrative of an expedition to the Zambesi and its tributaries. (John Murray, 1865)*

Bothwell and Uddingston

Duncan, Robert. Bothwellhaugh: a Lanarkshire mining community 1884-1965. (Workers Educational Association and Bothwellhaugh Ex-Residents Committee, 1986)

Henderson, George and Waddell, J. Jeffrey. By Bothwell Banks. (D. Hobbs and Co., 1904)

Jamieson, David. Uddingston in old picture postcards. (European Library, 1984)

Jamieson, David. Uddingston the village: a history of Uddingston and District. Parts 1-5. (D. Jamieson and others, 1972-83)

McPhillips, John. Doon the hill - up the hill. (Scottish and Universal Newspapers Ltd., 1986)

Pagan, John S. The antiquities of Bothwell. (James McKelvie and Sons, 1892)

Simpson, W. Douglas. Bothwell Castle. 3rd. edition with amendments, revised by D.J. Breeze and J.R. Hume. (Historic Scotland, 1990)

Stenlake, Richard. Bygone Uddingston. (Stenlake and McCourt, 1989)

Walks around Bothwell. (Bothwell Village Association, 1984)

Larkhall

Bulloch, Robert. A century of economic striving: a history of the inception, aspirations, progress and personalities of the Larkhall Victualling Society (established 1821). (S.C.W.S.Ltd., 1922)

McLellan, Jack. Larkhall: its historical development. (H. Matthews and Co., 1979)

McWhirter, M. T. Old Larkie landmarks. (Hamilton Advertiser, n.d.)

Notes on the Larkhall Building Societies. (Larkhall Heritage Group, 1990)

Stenlake, Richard. Bygone Larkhall. (Richard Stenlake, 1992)

Stonehouse

Naismith, Robert. Stonehouse, historical and traditional. (Robert Forrester, 1885)

Stenlake, Richard. Bygone Stonehouse. (Richard Stenlake, 1994)

Wilson, George F. Hame. (Privately printed, 1969)

Young, John R. The historical sites of Stonehouse. (Stonehouse Heritage Group, 1994)

Cameronians

Cameronians (Scottish Rifles) 300 years of service 1689-1989. (c.1989)

Carter, Thomas. (ed.) Historical record of the Twenty-Sixth or Cameronian Regiment. (Byfield, Stanford and Co., 1867)

Crichton, Andrew. Life and diary of Lt. Col. John Blackader, Deputy Governor of Stirling Castle. (Edinburgh, 1825)

History of the Cameronians (Scottish Rifles). Four volume official history as listed below.

Johnston, S.H.F. The history of the Cameronians (Scottish Rifles) Vol. I 1689-1910. (Gale and Polden, 1957)

Story, Colonel H.H. The history of the Cameronians (Scottish Rifles) Vol. II 1910-1933. (Hazell Watson and Viney, 1961)

Barclay, Brigadier C.N. The history of the Cameronians (Scottish Rifles) Vol. III 1933-1946. (Sifton Praed, 1947)

Baynes, John. The history of the Cameronians (Scottish Rifles). Vol. IV The close of Empire 1948-1968. (Cassell, 1971)

Covenanters

Hamilton Old Parish Church Bicentary Report 1734-1934. (1934)

Hewison, James King. The Covenanters. 2 volumes. (John Smith and Son, rev. ed.,1913)

Niven, Thomas Eric. East Kilbride: the history of parish and village. (Gavin Watson Ltd., 2nd. ed., 1988)

Thomson, Rev. John H. The martyr graves of Scotland. (Johnstone, Hunter and Co., 1875)

Mining

Arnot, R. Page. A history of the Scottish miners from the earliest times. (George Allen & Unwin, 1955)

Campbell, Alan B. The Lanarkshire miners: a social history of their trade unions 1775-1974. (John Donald, 1979)

Memoirs of the Geological Survey, Scotland. The economic geology of the central coalfield of Scotland. Local volumes include:-

Area VII Rutherglen, Hamilton and Wishaw. (H.M.S.O., 1920)

Area VIII East Kilbride and Quarter. (H.M.S.O., 1917)

Area IX Carluke, Strathaven and Larkhall. (H.M.S.O., 1921)

National Coal Board. *A short history of the Scottish coal-mining industry. (National Coal Board, 1958)*

Report on the Blantyre Colliery Explosion 1877...with Minutes of Evidence...21st December 1877. [C.1916] (H.M.S.O., 1878)

Report....Circumstances attending an explosion at Udston Colliery,

Hamilton on the 28th May 1887. [C.5192] (H.M.S.O., 1887)

Wallace, William. *Some notes on the coal industry in Hamilton. (Bell College, 1985)*

Textiles

British Parliamentary Papers

A Copy of Instructions issued to Assistant Commissioners of Inquiry into Hand-Loom Weavers. BPP. 1837-38 (212) XLV.

Hand Loom Weavers, Assistant Commissioner's Report from South of Scotland. BPP. 1839 (195) XLII.

Royal Commission... Poor Laws in Scotland. Minutes of Evidence... Lowland Counties. BPP. 1844 (565) XXII.I.

Lochhead, Jessie H. *Lace-making in Hamilton. (Hamilton Public Libraries and Museum Committee, 1971)*

Murray, Norman. *The Scottish hand-loom weavers 1790-1850: a social history. (John Donald, 1978)*

Walker, Gavin. *Hand-loom weaving in Hamilton and District. (Hamilton District Libraries and Museum, 1976)*

Young, John R. *The Stanis Weavers: a history of weaving in Stonehouse 1750-1890. (Stonehouse Heritage Group, 1993)*

Other useful information sources include directories, newspapers, Ordnance Survey maps and microfilm census returns of local parishes from 1841-1891.

Should you wish further information or advice on local history sources please contact the Reference and Local Studies Department, Hamilton Central Library, 98 Cadzow Street, Hamilton. Tel. 01698-894044 Ext. 2403.